Table of Contents

INSTRUCTIONS 5
  STUDENT PROGRESS RECORD 6
    CREATION (Book 1) 7
    THE FALL OF MAN (Book 2) 8
    JESUS (Book 3) 9
    FORGIVE (Book 4) 10
    YOUR POWER IN JESUS (Book 5) 11
    THE KINGDOM OF GOD (Book 6) 12
    FRUIT OF THE SPIRIT 13

CREATION (Read Book 1) 15
  PARENT LETTER 1 16
  FOLLOW UP ACTIVITIES 17
    THE THANK YOU GAME! 18
    GIVING THANKS AND PRAISE! 19
    MAKE A PRAISE BANNER! 20
    THE LORD'S PRAYER 22
      CELL PHONE 25
    TALKING WITH FATHER 26
      CARDS TEMPLATES 27
    WHAT DID GOD SAY? LESSON 1 28
      TO KNOW GOD'S WORD 30
      LEARNING SCRIPTURES FOR OUR BOOKS 30
    FINDING SEEDS 34
    DO YOU KNOW HOW MUCH FATHER LOVES YOU? 36

THE FALL OF MAN (Read Book 2) 38
  PARENT LETTER 2 39
  FOLLOW UP ACTIVITIES 40
    I CHOOSE GOD! 41
    PRAYING TO FATHER 42
    SPIRIT, SOUL, AND BODY 43
    WHICH KINGDOM DO YOU CHOOSE? 45
    TELL ME SOMETHING GOOD! 47
    GOD CANNOT LIE! 48
      THE TRUTH OR A LIE STATEMENTS 50
    CHOOSE! 52
    THE LAWS OF THE KINGDOM! 56
    WHAT DID GOD SAY? LESSON 2 58
      TO KNOW GOD'S WORD 59
      LEARNING SCRIPTURES FOR OUR BOOKS 61

JESUS (Read Book 3) 64
  PARENT LETTER 3 65
  FOLLOW UP ACTIVITIES 67
    I'M A CHILD OF GOD!   LET'S CELEBRATE! 68
    CERTIFICATE OF THE DAY I BELIEVED IN JESUS 69
    JESUS OUR SUPER HERO! 70
      MAKING A SUPER LOVE T-SHIRT: 72

IDEAS FOR CHILDREN TO PRACTICE LOVE:	72
COMMUNION JESUS IS OUR BREAD OF LIFE	73
THE BREAD	73
THE GRAPE JUICE	74
I HAVE ETERNAL LIFE TO LIVE FOREVER!	75
WHAT DID GOD SAY? LESSON 3	78
AWESOME HOLY SPIRIT!	84
FATHER, SON, and HOLY SPIRIT!	86

FORGIVE (Read Book 4) 88

PARENT LETTER 4	**89**
FOLLOW UP ACTIVITIES	**90**
FATHER HAS FORGIVEN ME SONG	91
THE FORGIVE EXERCISE!	92
YOU ARE A KING AND AMBASSADOR	99
FRUIT OF THE SPIRIT	102
WHAT DID GOD SAY? LESSON 4	106
TO KNOW GOD'S WORD	107
LEARNING SCRIPTURES FOR OUR BOOKS	109
CONSEQUENCES	111
FORGIVING OTHERS	114

YOUR POWER IN JESUS (Read Book 5) 117

PARENT LETTER 5	**118**
FOLLOW UP ACTIVITIES	**119**
LEARNING GOD'S WORD	120
THE THRONE ROOM	121
THE POWER IN YOUR WORDS	122
WHAT DID GOD SAY? LESSON 5	124
TO KNOW GOD'S WORD	125
LEARNING SCRIPTURES FOR OUR BOOKS	127
HOW TO CHANGE YOUR THOUGHTS	130
WHY THE DEVIL DOES NOT WANT YOU TO PRAY IN TONGUES!	133

THE KINGDOM OF GOD (Read Book 6) 135

PARENT LETTER 6	**136**
FOLLOW UP ACTIVITIES	**137**
A SONG ABOUT LOVE!	138
MY BOOK OF LOVE TO GIVE FATHER GLORY!	139
WHAT DID GOD SAY? LESSON 6	142
TO KNOW GOD'S WORD	143
LEARNING SCRIPTURES FOR OUR BOOKS	145
MY PRAYER BAG	147
DON'T BE AFRAID!	149
SHOWING GOD'S KINGDOM	153
I HAVE A PURPOSE!	155
I HAVE A PURPOSE CERTIFICATE	156

SONGS FOR YOU TO SING WITH CHILDREN 157

THE PRAYER SONG	158
I SAY I LOVE YOU Father	158

I CHOOSE GOD!	159
I LOVE YOU JESUS	159
THANK YOU JESUS!	160
HOLY SPIRIT HELPS ME LOVE!	160
THE FRUIT OF THE SPIRIT SONG!	160
JESUS WILL NEVER LEAVE ME	161
HOLY SPIRIT HELPS ME DO THINGS RIGHT	161
GOOD THOUGHTS	162
THIS IS WHAT I CAN DO	162
I LOVE YOU	163
JESUS IS HIS NAME	163
FORGIVE	163
LISTEN	164
I CHOSE JESUS	165
I RECEIVED HOLY SPIRIT	165
JESUS IS MY SUPER HERO!	166
YES, MY FATHER LOVES ME!	166
JESUS IS MY FRIEND	167
GRACE	168
CAN YOU PRAY TODAY?	169

APPENDIX 170

Now What Do I Do? 170
And Where Do I Begin? 170

ROOM SET-UP	171
FREE CHOICE CENTERS	172
POSITIVE GUIDANCE	172
DAILY SCHEDULE	173
CHILDREN'S ARRIVAL/FREEPLAY	174
TRANSITION	174
CIRCLE	175
FOLLOW-UP ACTIVITIES	176
CLEAN UP	176
RESTROOM/TRANSITION TO SNACK	176
PRAYER/SNACK/CLEAN-UP	177
FREEPLAY/PARENT PICK-UP	177
STUDENT PROGRESS RECORD	177
KINGDOM OF GOD RULE	178
QUESTIONS AND ANSWERS	179

HOLY BIBLE SCRIPTURE REFERENCES 189

"CREATION" SCRIPTURE REFERENCES 190
"THE FALL OF MAN" SCRIPTURE REFERENCES 192
"JESUS" SCRIPTURE REFERENCES 194
"FORGIVE" SCRIPTURE REFERENCES 196
"YOUR POWER IN JESUS" SCRIPTURE REFERENCES 198
"THE KINGDOM OF GOD" SCRIPTURE REFERENCE" 200

INSTRUCTIONS

Foundation Curriculum Contents: Six (6) Storybook Lessons,
and one (1) Foundation Curriculum Activities Manual

Read each story book lesson in sequence (from 1- 6)

1) **Run a copy of a Student Progress Record for each child located in the Foundation Curriculum Activities Manual.**

2) **Select a Follow-Up Activity to reinforce the book you are teaching.**
   (Example: For the timeframe you teach from the "Creation" book, select your Follow-Up Activities from that section of the Foundation Curriculum Activities Manual).

3) **Read the book aloud to the child/ren showing the pictures and listening to answers.**
   (Plan to read the same book a minimum of three to six times during the time frame needed to help children understand the objectives listed in the Student Progress Record and at the back of each book).

4) **After reading, guide the child/ren to complete the Follow up Activity.**

5) **Assess the understanding of each child based on:**
   a. The content of their answers to the questions in the story and the Follow up Activities.
   b. Document the child's progress on their Student Progress Record.

6) **Throughout the week/s that you choose to remain on the same story book lesson, encourage discussion and retelling of the story by the children, and; complete a different Follow-up Activity from the section in which you are teaching.**

7) **If curriculum is taught in a setting away from home**
   (i.e. a school or church): Send home a copy of the book, Parent Letter (for the book you are teaching) and a Follow-Up Activity for parents to reinforce the teaching with their child at home. Discuss progress with parents and update the Student Progress Record accordingly.

8) **When you determine that the child/ren understand all of the objectives for the book you are teaching, begin the next Story Book Lesson.**

HAVE QUESTIONS?   EMAIL: info@abc-Jesus.com

P.A.C.E.
www.ABC-Jesus.com
© All Rights Reserved

STUDENT PROGRESS RECORD

Student Name: _____

It is important that individual progress is assessed, recorded and monitored to ensure each child understands and practices the foundational knowledge of:
1) God's love
2) Their "Born Again" identity,
3) And power and authority in Christ Jesus!

Directions:
1) Copy one Student Progress Record per child to track each child's progress.
2) After each lesson, assess the student's understanding of the objectives based on your observations. If the child "Fully Understands" the objective, score a + rating and write the date that the objective was rated.
3) For any - rating, use the Recommended Follow up Activities or plan other activities to help the child fully understand the objective.
4) If a child has a - score and you later assess that the child has gained a full understanding, change the score to a + rating.
5) On the last two pages of this Student Progress Record, write what you or someone else saw the child doing that showed the Fruit of the Spirit of God in them. such as:

   - ✓ Love
   - ✓ Patience
   - ✓ Faithfulness
   - ✓ Joy
   - ✓ Kindness
   - ✓ Humility
   - ✓ Peace
   - ✓ Goodness
   - ✓ Self Control

   Be sure to tell the child when you see them showing the Fruit of the Spirit. (Galatians 5:22-23)

6) Plan to help children make-up any missed lesson.

THANK YOU AND GOD BLESS YOU FOR HELPING CHILDREN TO KNOW GOD AS FATHER, JESUS AS SAVIOR AND FRIEND, AND HOLY SPIRIT AS HELPER!

Score a Rating of ✚ if Child "Fully Understands"

Score a Rating of ▬ if Child Does "Not Yet" Understand

P.A.C.E.
www.ABC-Jesus.com
© All Rights Reserved

STUDENT PROGRESS RECORD
CREATION (Book 1)

Student Name: _____

OBJECTIVES TO BE UNDERSTOOD	SCORE	DATE	Recommended Follow-Up Activities
1) God is your heavenly Father.			☐ The Lord's Prayer
2) Heavenly Father is a Spirit and is Holy.			☐ Reread CREATION (Book 1)
3) Father loves you!			☐ Talking with Father ☐ Reread CREATION (Book 1) ☐ Do you know how much Father loves you?
4) Father will talk with you in Prayer.			☐ The Lord's Prayer ☐ Talking with Father
5) Father made everything by His Word that is alive and true.			☐ What Did God Say? Lesson 1
6) Father put the seed inside animals, birds, fish, fruits, vegetables and plants for everything to have babies and grow again from the seed in it. All people were born from the seed inside the first man Adam.			☐ Finding Seeds ☐ Reread CREATION (Book 1)
7) Father made you to be like Him. To understand His Words are alive and true, and see God's Word like a sword; practice speaking His Words that give life. To hide God's Word in your heart and declare it. And watch God do what He said.			☐ What Did God Say? Lesson 1
8) Heavenly Father has blessed you so thank Him. • There are different ways to give thanks and praise. • Father deserves to be praised and given thanks by you.			☐ The Thank You Game ☐ Giving Thanks and Praise ☐ Make A Praise Banner

P.A.C.E.
www.ABC-Jesus.com
© All Rights Reserved

STUDENT PROGRESS RECORD
THE FALL OF MAN (Book 2)

Student Name:_____

OBJECTIVES TO BE UNDERSTOOD	SCORE	DATE	Recommended Follow-Up Activities
1) You are a spirit and a living soul; your spirit and soul live in your body; your spirit and soul do not die, but live forever with whomever you choose to believe, either God or the devil.			☐ Spirit, Soul and Body ☐ Reread THE FALL OF MAN (Book 2)
2) The bad angels got kicked out of heaven and now there is a very bad devil on the earth.			☐ Which Kingdom Do You Choose?
3) Your heavenly Father has a kingdom, and satan has a kingdom, and you have a choice as to which kingdom you will serve.			☐ Which Kingdom Do You Choose? ☐ I Choose God (song)! ☐ Choose!
4) God made laws that He will not break.			☐ The Laws of the Kingdom!
5) Heavenly Father loves you even when you disobey.			☐ The Laws of the Kingdom!
6) It is important to choose to listen and obey God.			☐ Praying To Father ☐ Tell Me Something Good! ☐ Choose!
7) God can not lie!			☐ God cannot lie!
8) You can know the difference between a lie of the devil versus the truth of God.			☐ God cannot lie! ☐ Reread THE FALL OF MAN (Book 2)
9) The devil tells lies and tries to trick people.			☐ God cannot lie!
10) You can pray in your own words to Father.			☐ Praying To Father
11) Father made you to be like Him. To understand His Words are alive and true, and see God's Word like a sword; practice speaking His Words that give life. To hide God's Word in your heart and declare it. And watch God do what He said.			☐ What Did God Say? Lesson 2 ☐ Reread THE FALL OF MAN (Book 2)

STUDENT PROGRESS RECORD
JESUS (Book 3)

Student Name: _____

OBJECTIVES TO BE UNDERSTOOD	SCORE	DATE	Recommended Follow-Up Activities
1) Jesus *chose* to let people hurt him and to die to save you from sin and death. Father raised Jesus from the dead by His Holy Spirit.			☐ Reread Jesus (Book 3)
2) Jesus descended to hell and beat the devil for you!			☐ Jesus, Our Super Hero
3) No one is greater than Father and Jesus. You can practice super love everyday when you show others love.			☐ Jesus, Our Super Hero ☐ Awesome Holy Spirit
4) Adam's seed became bad, but you can be "Born Again" by the good seed in Jesus.			☐ Reread Jesus (Book 3)
5) The day you were "Born Again" is a special and important day to remember.			☐ I am a child of God! Let's Celebrate! ☐ Certificate
6) You can pray to receive Jesus as your Lord and Savior (your daily bread), and remember Him with communion.			☐ Communion ☐ Reread Jesus (Book 3)
7) You can pray and ask to receive the gift of Holy Spirit. Holy Spirit helps you.			☐ Awesome Holy Spirit!
8) You can choose to speak in an unknown tongue.			☐ Awesome Holy Spirit!
9) When you believe Jesus, you don't have to die, but can live with heavenly Father and Jesus who loves you forever.			☐ I Have Eternal Life to Live Forever! Fun Things to Do With Father and Jesus ☐ Spirit, Soul and Body (See Lesson 2)
10) Father made you to be like Him. To understand His Words are alive and true, and see God's Word like a sword; practice speaking His Words that give life. To hide God's Word in your heart and declare it. And watch God do what He said.			☐ What Did God Say? Lesson 3
11) Father, Son and Holy Spirit are One God.			☐ Father, Son, and Holy Spirit!

STUDENT PROGRESS RECORD
FORGIVE (Book 4)

Student Name: _____

OBJECTIVES TO BE UNDERSTOOD	SCORE	DATE	Recommended Follow-Up Activities
1) Father has forgiven all of your sins because of Jesus!			☐ Father has forgiven me (song)
2) You can set your mind on the things of the Spirit and be led by the Holy Spirit of Jesus and bring forth the Fruit of the Spirit.			☐ Fruit of the Spirit ☐ Student Progress Record (see Pages 13 and 14)
3) You are a child of God, a king and ambassador for Jesus! You are a leader to show love to others.			☐ Reread FORGIVE (Book 4) ☐ You are a king and ambassador
4) In your spirit you are one with Jesus and heavenly Father.			☐ Awesome Holy Spirit (See Lesson 3)
5) Heavenly Father and Jesus commanded you to forgive every one. If you do not forgive others God will not forgive you.			☐ The Forgive Exercise ☐ Consequences ☐ Forgive Others
6) Because you are love like Jesus and Father, love FORGIVES others.			☐ Reread FORGIVE (Book 4) ☐ The Forgive Exercise
7) Father made you to be like Him. To understand His Words are alive and true, and see God's Word like a sword; practice speaking His Words that give life. To hide God's Word in your heart and declare it. And watch God do what He said He would do.			☐ What Did God Say? Lesson 4 ☐ Reread FORGIVE (Book 4)

P.A.C.E.
www.ABC-Jesus.com
© All Rights Reserved

STUDENT PROGRESS RECORD
YOUR POWER IN JESUS (Book 5)

Student Name: _____

OBJECTIVES TO BE UNDERSTOOD	SCORE	DATE	Recommended Follow-Up Activities
1) Because of Jesus you can come boldly into your Father's Throne Room of Grace, receive God's grace, and pray to Father.			☐ The Throne Room ☐ Reread YOUR POWER IN JESUS (Book 5)
2) To think *new* like heavenly Father and Jesus by understanding God's Word, and have fun learning God's Word.			☐ Learning God's Word! ☐ Reread YOUR POWER IN JESUS, (Book 5)
3) You can change bad thoughts to good thoughts. God's living Word has life and light in it and will remove the darkness of any lie or bad thought.			☐ How to Change Your Thoughts
4) Your words contain the power of death and life in them.			☐ The Power in Your Words ☐ Tell Me Something Good (See Lesson 2)
5) God's Word is a sword that cuts through everything.			☐ Reread YOUR POWER IN JESUS (Book 5)
6) Father made you to be like Him. To understand His Words are alive and true, and see God's Word like a sword; practice speaking His Words that give life. To hide God's Word in your heart and declare it. And watch God do what He said He would do.			☐ What Did God Say? Lesson 5 ☐ Why The Devil Does Not Want You to Pray in Tongues!

P.A.C.E.
www.ABC-Jesus.com
© All Rights Reserved

STUDENT PROGRESS RECORD
THE KINGDOM OF GOD (Book 6)

Student Name: _____

OBJECTIVES TO BE UNDERSTOOD	SCORE	DATE	Recommended Follow-Up Activities
1) You can show Father's *Kingdom* of Love on earth, like Jesus.			☐ My book of love to give God glory ☐ Showing God's Kingdom
2) Jesus is called God's Word. He only said and did what Father said. No one has more *Power* than Father!			☐ Reread THE KINGDOM OF GOD (Book 6)
3) You can give Father Honor and *Glory* like Jesus when you show God's love to others. You can pray for things important to God, and when you pray with someone who agrees with you, it is powerful!			☐ A Song About Love! ☐ My Prayer Bag!
4) Holy Spirit helps you to show others God's love.			☐ Awesome Holy Spirit (See Lesson 3)
5) When you believe Jesus, you can use His name when you pray and to heal the sick, raise the dead, and make demons leave.			☐ Reread THE KINGDOM OF GOD (Book 6) ☐ Don't Be Afraid!
6) Father made you to be like Him. To understand His Words are alive and true, and see God's Word like a sword; practice speaking His Words that give life. To hide God's Word in your heart and declare it. And watch God do what He said He would do. God has given you a purpose and will speak to you.			☐ What Did God Say? Lesson 6 ☐ Reread THE KINGDOM OF GOD (Book 6) ☐ My Purpose

P.A.C.E.
www.ABC-Jesus.com
© All Rights Reserved

STUDENT PROGRESS RECORD
FRUIT OF THE SPIRIT

Student Name: _____

Observe, Record and Tell the child when you or someone else see them practicing and showing the Fruit of the Spirit.

Galatians 5:22-23 (An example of telling the child could be: "I like how you were **kind** to __ when you let her…..")

Fruit of Spirit Observed	Date of Observation	Description of what the child did to show Love
Love		
Love		
Love		

Fruit of Spirit Observed	Date of Observation	Description of what the child did to show Joy
Joy		
Joy		
Joy		

Fruit of Spirit Observed	Date of Observation	Description of what the child did to show Peace
Peace		
Peace		
Peace		

Fruit of Spirit Observed	Date of Observation	Description of what the child did to show Patience
Patience		
Patience		
Patience		

FRUIT OF THE SPIRIT (continued):

Fruit of Spirit Observed	Date of Observation	Description of what the child did to show Kindness
Kindness		
Kindness		
Kindness		

Fruit of Spirit Observed	Date of Observation	Description of what the child did to show Goodness
Goodness		
Goodness		
Goodness		

Fruit of Spirit Observed	Date of Observation	Description of what the child did to show Faithfulness
Faithfulness		
Faithfulness		
Faithfulness		

Fruit of Spirit Observed	Date of Observation	Description of what the child did to show Humility
Humility		
Humility		
Humility		

Fruit of Spirit Observed	Date of Observation	Description of what the child did to show Self-Control
Self-Control		
Self-Control		
Self-Control		

CREATION
(Read Book 1)

PARENT LETTER 1

Dear Parents,

We have been given a command from God to teach our children about Him. God said, "And you shall love the LORD your God with all your heart, and with all your soul, and with all your might. And these words which I command you this day shall be in your heart and you shall teach them diligently to your children, and shall talk of them when you sit in your house and when you walk by the way, and when you lie down, and when you rise up."
(Deuteronomy 6:5-7; Mark 12:28-31)

We have chosen the Foundation Curriculum to partner with you to show your child how much God loves them, their true identity, and their authority and power in Christ Jesus. Your part is to read and reread our curriculum's story several times to your young child and encourage the child to retell the story. Older children may choose to read or tell the story to you and others, but remember to ask them questions from the story book lessons.

Book 1, CREATION, focuses on God's love for His children and how He made the earth ready for us. Our response to our Father in heaven, who loves us, should be heartfelt gratitude and thankfulness. Therefore we ask that you give time each day to informally talk about and give praise and thanks to heavenly Father for the good things He has done for you. For all good things come from God!
(James 1:17)

We've included Follow Up Activities to practice thanking God. For example, the Thank You Game is a simple and fun activity that the whole family can get involved in playing anytime during the day or before bedtime. Be blessed as you teach your child to think about and see the goodness and love of God everywhere!
(Psalm 50:23)

If you have any questions as we begin this spiritual journey together, please contact me.

Sincerely in Christ,

Your Child's Teacher
Contact information: _____

Scriptural References: Isaiah 43; Isaiah 53; John 3:15-17; John 17:20-23; Isaiah 49:16

P.A.C.E.
www.ABC-Jesus.com
© All Rights Reserved

FOLLOW UP ACTIVITIES

FOLLOW UP ACTIVITY
THE THANK YOU GAME!

Objectives to be Understood: For children to practice thinking about how much heavenly Father has blessed them and to express why they are thankful to Him.

Materials: None

Rules: The game can be played with as few as two persons or as many people that want to play. Each person has a turn one at a time naming:
- *One thing or person for which they are thankful to heavenly Father, and why they are thankful for it.*

As the game progresses and the child/ren think of many things they are thankful for and why they are thankful:
- *Increase the second round to naming two things per person;*
- *During the third round, name three things for which they are thankful to heavenly Father, etc.*

The children can name the same thing that someone else has named since they also have to tell why they are thankful.

When a player can't think of something or someone, they forfeit their turn, and it's the next person's turn.

Continue playing until players lose interest or until the time frame determined to end the game arrives.

Scriptures:
I Thessalonians 5:17-18; Luke 6:12; Luke 11:1; Ephesians 6:18; Colossians 4:2

FOLLOW UP ACTIVITY
GIVING THANKS AND PRAISE!

Objectives to be Understood:
1) There are different ways to give thanks and praise, and;
2) To practice giving thanks and praise to God!

Materials: Set out materials such as: paper, markers, crayons, pencils, glue, scissors, streamers (for dancing or let child choose use), musical instruments (such as bells, play guitar, tambourine), etc.

Parent/Teacher Script:
When you thank God, it lets Him know that you appreciate what He has done for you. When good things happen to you, know that it is always your heavenly Father because He only does good things, so remember to thank Him! Let's each thank Him now! I'll start. Father, I thank you for _____. Does anyone else want to thank heavenly Father?

Praise blesses and glorifies your heavenly Father! Can you think of some ways that you can offer your heavenly Father thanks, praise and worship?

Here are some ideas:

- You could write a love letter or a poem and read it to Him-- that's praise from your heart and your mouth.
- You can make up a beautiful new song and sing it to Him.
- You can thank God and let Him know that you appreciate His love to you and others.
- You could bow down and worship Him and say wonderful words to Him that you think of from your heart, like Alleluia!
- You can worship Him by lifting up your hands to Him and singing or talking to Him.
- You can move your body in a beautiful dance before Him in praise to His Holy name.
- You can draw your heavenly Father a picture of things you like and enjoy that He has created. Then speak to Him with your words to say how much you appreciate Him for creating all things.
- Rejoice and talk about your God! Your heavenly Father loves you! So think of what you want to do to give heavenly Father your love with thanks, praise and worship!

After you make or plan something, if you want to share, we will thank and praise God with you for your special gift to Him!

Scriptures:
James 1:17; I Thessalonians 5:18; Psalm 34:1, 50:23; Psalm 145:21; Psalm 149:1; Psalm 136:1; Psalm 95:6; Revelation 19:1; Psalm 134:2; Psalm 149:3; Psalm 107-21-22

FOLLOW UP ACTIVITY
MAKE A PRAISE BANNER!

Objectives to be Understood: Heavenly Father deserves to be praised and thanked because He is God!

Materials: Poster board cut in rectangular shapes for banners (see examples below), praise words written on index cards, glue sticks, glitter, markers, stick-on or pre-cut letters of the praise words that will fit on the banner. Examples are:

HALLELUJAH!

GREAT IS OUR GOD!

GOD IS HOLY!

PRAISE GOD'S NAME!

GOD IS GOOD!

GLORY TO GOD!

MAKE A PRAISE BANNER *continued*

Instructions: Talk to children about the things God made for us in creation and why everyone should thank and praise God. Let children know they can make a Praise Banner to put in their home to remind them to say praises to God!

- Show children the praise to God words from the examples.
- Encourage children to choose the praise to God words that they want to put on their banner!
- Place the stick-on or pre-cut letters of the praise words where children can reach them.
- Ask each child to choose the letters of the praise words that they want to put on their banner and say to God.

For Children that do Not Know How to Spell the Praise Words:
Give the child an index card or piece of paper that has their chosen praise written on it.

- Give each child a rectangular poster board strip as their banner (see example).
- Children stick-on or glue the letters on the banner.
- Children can decorate their banner and praise words with stickers, glitter, markers, etc.
- Encourage the children who want to share to show their finished banner and tell why they want to praise God with the words they chose.
- Ask each child: where do you plan to hang your banner (in your home) to remind you to praise God?

Scriptures:
Revelation 7:12; 5:12-13; 4:8-11; 19:1; Psalm 150:6

FOLLOW UP ACTIVITY
THE LORD'S PRAYER

Objectives to be Understood: For children to know that God is their Father in heaven who hears their prayers and will talk with them, and; for children to practice talking to Father on a pretend cell phone.

Materials: Run a copy for each child of:
1) The Lord's Prayer (see template entitled The Lord's Prayer), and
2) Cell Phone (see template entitled Cell Phone). Other Materials include: Poster board- enough poster board for each child to glue one cell phone cut-out upon (see size of Cell Phone on template), scissors, crayons, markers, glue.

Parent/Teacher Script:
Did you know that prayer is talking with God?
(Listen to Responses)

To pray and talk with God means that when you believe Him, you can talk to Him and say words from your heart to Him, and He hears you. Do you understand? (Listen to Responses) God hears your prayer and speaks to you in your heart which is inside of you. You can talk to God, your heavenly Father about anything. When He talks to you, it's your turn to listen and hear Him. When you want to pray, go to your room or to a place by yourself and close the door to pray to your heavenly Father in secret. Father will see you and reward you.

When God's Son, Jesus was on the earth, he would go to a secret place away from everyone to pray to Father in heaven. He would talk and listen to Father about things that God told him to do. Jesus talked to his Father about how he felt and Father always helped him. Jesus would thank his Father for the power to do good things. One day Jesus was praying and talking with God. When Jesus finished praying, one of his friends asked him to teach them how to pray. So you will get a copy of what Jesus taught his friends. Some people call this the Lord's Prayer.
(Distribute copies of "The Lord's Prayer", see page 24)

Let's read it together.

(Read "The Lord's Prayer" together BEFORE continuing with the Parent/Teacher Script)
(After Reading Lord's Prayer Continue)

When Jesus said to pray and say, Our Father in heaven, who was Jesus telling you to pray to?
(Listen to Responses)

Jesus was telling you to pray and speak words from your heart to God your Father who lives in heaven! Jesus wants you to pray always and talk to Father like He did.

P.A.C.E.
www.ABC-Jesus.com
© All Rights Reserved

THE LORD'S PRAYER (continued):

Have you ever talked to someone on the telephone? When you talk on the telephone the person who you are talking to is sometimes far away and you can't see them. But you can hear their voice and they can hear your voice. Talking to God your heavenly Father is like talking to someone on a telephone, but God is close when you call Him. You do NOT need a telephone to pray and talk with your heavenly Father. You can simply talk with Him any time you choose. Do you think you have to scream or talk loud for Father to hear you? No, you do not have to talk loud or scream. Father can hear you when you whisper or speak softly to Him. He can even hear you when you pray in your heart.

We are going to make a pretend cell phone to practice praying and talking with Father on it. Do you think you need a cell phone to talk with God in heaven? (Listen to Responses)
No, you DO NOT need a cell phone to pray and talk with God. Remember, you can talk with God, your Father, any place and any time you choose! But the best place is alone with Him. When you pray to God your Father, like Jesus said, will God hear you?
Yes, Father will hear you when you believe Him and talk to Him from your heart! Let's practice talking with God and calling Him Father. Think about what you will say to God, your heavenly Father on your pretend cell phone.

Instructions: (To make a pretend cell phone)
- Give each child a copy of the cell phone from the template entitled Cell Phone.
- Child to cut out their cell phone picture. Help as needed.
- Give each child one cut-out cell phone shape from the poster board.
- Child to glue their cell phone picture onto the poster board cut-out.
- Child can color the back of their cell phone (poster board).
- Parent/Teacher instructs the children that finish making their cell phones to find a place in the room to begin to talk to Father.
- Ask: Does anyone want to share what you talked to your heavenly Father about?

Scriptures:
Psalm 3:4; 4:3-4; 91:14-16; John 10:27; Deuteronomy 6:6; Matthew 6:6-13; I John 5:13-15; Luke 6:12; John 17:1-26; Mark 8:6; Luke 11:1-4

The Lord's Prayer

*Our Father in heaven,
We pray that Your Name
will always be kept holy.
We pray that Your kingdom will come,
That what You want will be done,
Here on earth, the same as in heaven.
Give us this day our daily bread.
Forgive our sins, just as we have forgiven
those who did wrong to us.
Lead us not into temptation,
But deliver us from the evil one.
For Yours is the kingdom, and the power,
and the glory, forever.*
Amen.

Luke 11:2-4; Matthew 6:9-13

CELL PHONE

FOLLOW UP ACTIVITY
TALKING WITH FATHER

Objectives to be Understood: For children to know God loves them, and; to think about and say what they could talk with Father about throughout the day.

Materials: CARDS, Scissors, Glue, Tag board, Chart paper, Markers

Instructions: (TO MAKE THE CARDS BEFORE THE ACTIVITY)
- Run one copy of CARDS from CARDS Template.
- Glue the CARDS onto a card stock type paper such as tag board.
- Allow enough time for glue on cards to dry completely.
- Cut out the CARDS.
- Write at top of a sheet of chart paper: THINGS I WILL SAY TO FATHER!

Parent/Teacher Script:
Did you know that God your heavenly Father loves you?
(Listen to Responses)

God loves you! And because He loves you, Father wants you to talk with Him all the time about everything. He wants you to know Him. The way you get to know Father is to pray and talk with Him. He said to pray without stopping. So we are going to think about some things we could say to God in the daytime and nighttime. We are going to play a thinking game. In this game you can see how many things you can think of to pray and say to your heavenly Father.

RULES:

1. Place the cards in a pile within easy reach of all.
2. A child pulls a card.
3. Parent/Teacher asks: WHAT COULD YOU SAY TO FATHER WHEN: Parent/Teacher or a child reads the rest of the question on the card.
4. Parent/Teacher to encourage children to answer and think of different things. Give ideas as needed.
5. If child has no answer, begin again at rule 2.
6. The parent/teacher is to write the children's responses on the chart paper. Post the chart where children can see it.

Scriptures:
I Thessalonians 5:17-18; I Timothy 2:8; Acts 10:2; Luke 22:32; Luke 18:1

P.A.C.E.
www.ABC-Jesus.com
© All Rights Reserved

CARDS TEMPLATES

WHAT COULD YOU SAY TO FATHER WHEN **YOU NEED SOMETHING?**	*WHAT COULD YOU SAY TO FATHER WHEN* **YOU GO TO BED AT NIGHT?**
WHAT COULD YOU SAY TO FATHER WHEN **YOU WANT TO TELL HIM A SECRET?**	*WHAT COULD YOU SAY TO FATHER WHEN* **YOU ARE HAPPY?**
WHAT COULD YOU SAY TO FATHER WHEN **YOU ARE AFRAID?**	*WHAT COULD YOU SAY TO FATHER WHEN* **YOU ARE SAD?**
WHAT COULD YOU SAY TO FATHER WHEN **YOU GET FOOD AND OTHER THINGS YOU NEED OR WANT?**	*WHAT COULD YOU SAY TO FATHER WHEN* **YOU WAKE UP IN THE MORNING?**

FOLLOW UP ACTIVITY
WHAT DID GOD SAY? LESSON 1

Objectives to be Understood: For children to know:
1) God made you to be like Him;
2) God's Word is alive and true;
3) God's Word is like a sword;
4) God's Word has the power of life in it, and;
5) to say what God has said.

Activity: Children will write in their books the Scriptures/Words God Said.

Important Note: This activity is included in each of our 6 lessons with a different scripture in each lesson for children to receive into their hearts.

Materials: For Introduction: Holy Bible and a second book (not a Bible);
Materials To Make A Book: Pencils; Markers; Stapler; Pre-made book template or purchased notebooks (see Preparation below)

Preparation: To MAKE A BOOK
Pre-make book templates for each child by folding two sheets of paper in half and stapling (two staples on the folded side so pages open like a book); OR purchase lined notebooks.
Write out and post (where children can easily see) the following scripture:

WE LOVE HIM BECAUSE HE FIRST LOVED US!
I John 4:19

WHAT DID GOD SAY? LESSON 1 (Continued):
(Hold up the Bible in one hand and another book in the other)

INTRODUCTION:

Parent/Teacher Script:
Did you know that these two books are different?
How are they different?
(Listen to Responses)

They both have words.
They both are made of paper.
They both have a front and a back cover.
The difference is the Bible is full of God's Words that are ALIVE and TRUE.
God's living words have POWER in them and can change things when you believe what God has said.
God made everything to be good and come alive by His Word.
Everything God says must happen! God can not lie.
The POWER in God's Words is sharp and cuts like a big SWORD.
Do you believe God's Word is true?
(Listen to responses)

God has given you His Words to believe Him and SAY WHAT GOD SAID.
Everything that God has said is for your good.
Do you know who God made you to be like?
(Listen to responses)

God made you to be like Him and say good words that give life.
This is why it is very important that you learn the things that God has said in the Bible.
Different writers wrote what God told them to write in the Bible. The Words in the Bible are called scriptures. The Bible has different parts called books. The scripture that we will learn today can be found in the book of I John the fourth chapter and the 19th verse. I John 4:19
The Bible has stories about God, and Words God said that are written down for you to know God and His love for you.

TO KNOW GOD'S WORD

First, you must LET YOUR EARS HEAR GOD'S WORD AND BELIEVE IT.
Second, LET YOUR MOUTH SAY THE WORDS THAT GOD HAS SAID.
Third, Tell your mind to THINK ABOUT WHAT GOD HAS SAID.
When you think about what God has said, HIS WORD GOES INSIDE YOUR HEART. And your heart will help you love like God.

LEARNING SCRIPTURES FOR OUR BOOKS

INSTRUCTIONS:

Parent/Teacher Script:
In our books, we will write scriptures or Words God said.
Our first scripture is: We love Him because He first loved us.
What do you think it means when God says,
WE LOVE HIM BECAUSE HE FIRST LOVED US?
(Listen to Responses)

Do you remember why God prepared the earth?
(Listen to Responses)

God prepared the earth for His children. Us!
Why do you think God created and made everything for His children?
Because God loved you before you were born. God loved you first!
This is why God said, WE LOVE HIM BECAUSE HE FIRST LOVED US!
(Distribute Books (Pre-made or Purchased Notebooks) to each child. See Preparation)

Your book is for you to write the scriptures you have learned that God has said. If you would like God, your heavenly Father, to help you to know Him and the Words He has said, you can pray and say these words after me, or you can pray to God in your own words. Ready.
Let's pray!

PRAYER

Father,
(Pause for Children to Repeat)
I want to know You
(Pause)
Will you help me?
(Pause)
I want to hear and believe You
(Pause)
Will You teach me to say
(Pause)
what You have said every day?
(Pause)
Thank You Father!
(Pause)
Will you help me
(Pause)
to think about Your Word?
(Pause)
Thank You Father!
(Pause)
Will You let Your Word
(Pause)
change my heart
(Pause)
so I will love like You?
(Pause)
Thank You for hearing me
(Pause)
and answering my prayer!
(Pause)
I love You!
(Pause)
Amen.

Parent/Teacher Script, (Continued)**:**

This time you can say the words after me.
We love Him (children repeat)
because (children repeat)
He first (children repeat)
loved us. (children repeat)

What do you think God means when He says to you:
You love Him because He first loved you?
(Listen to responses)

God loves you! God loved you first. He is the one who thought about you and made you for Himself. No one can love you like God. So now you can choose to believe Him and love Him back.

Let's say it boldly together again:
We love Him because He first loved us!

Let's say it again:
We love Him because He first loved us!
Have you ever had someone tell you they love you?
(Listen to responses)

Your Father in heaven loves you with a love that is not like the love on earth. His love is called agape love. Agape love is a heavenly amazing love.

Repeat after me.
God loves me (children repeat)
with His agape love. (children repeat)
Did you know that God's love is true?
(Listen to responses)

It is so true that the more you say that God loves you and you think about how much God loves you, the power in God's words will go into your heart to live. And you will know the truth. And the truth is God loves you!

Let's say the scripture together again.
We love Him (pause)
because (pause)
He first (pause)
loved us. (repeat)

Write God's Words in your book.
Everyday declare or say God's Words so your ears can Hear His Words! You can read your book out loud so you can hear the words!

Parent/Teacher Script, (continued)**:**

Every day pay attention and watch God do what He said because you believed Him, and you said what He said. When you see that God has done what He said, write or draw a picture in your book about the good things God did for you. And come tell us about it.

(If children are using notebooks)
You can take your book home but remember to bring it back so you can write more Words that God said in it.

LET'S SING THESE WORDS GOD SAID:
(Sing to the tune of "If you're happy and you know it")
(make up motions to do with song)

We love Him because He first loved us! Halleluiah!
We love Him because He first loved us! Halleluiah!
We love Him Yes we love Him.
We love Him Yes we love Him.
We love Him because He first loved us!
(DECLARE!)
Father loved us first!
(Repeat)

SONG: GOD LOVES ME!
(Sung to the tune of Barney Song)
(Do motions to Song)

YOU LOVE ME!
(Point upward, then to self)
I LOVE YOU!
(Point to self and upward)
YOU MAKE MY HEART GO PITTER-PAT!
(Point up, touch heart, Clap hands as you say pitter-pat)
YOU LOVED ME FIRST
(Point upward, then to self)
AND I LOVE YOU BACK!
(Kiss your hands and blow kisses up to Father)
YOU MAKE MY HEART GO PITTER-PAT!
(Point up, touch your heart, then clap hands as you say pitter-pat)
I LOVE YOU FATHER!
(Lift both hands up and SHOUT)

Scriptures:
I John 4:19; Hebrews 4:12; Isaiah 51:15-16; Jeremiah 1:9; Psalm 119:11; Proverbs 4:20-24

FOLLOW UP ACTIVITY
FINDING SEEDS

Objectives to be Understood: For children to know,

1) Father put the seed inside of animals, birds, fish, fruit, and plants for everything to have babies and grow again from the seed in it, and;
2) all people were born from the seed inside the first man Adam.

MATERIALS: Paper plates (one per child), Pencils, Markers, Crayons, Ribbon.

PREPARATION BEFORE TEACHING:
Draw two lines across the center of the paper plate to divide the plate into quarters, like a pie cut into four sections. Optional: Bring different types of seeds to show.

Parent/Teacher Script:
Ask the children:
Have you ever seen a seed inside of an apple or an orange? What are some other fruits that you have seen seeds inside of?
(Listen to Responses. Help children identify other fruits with seeds.)

Does an apple seed and a peach seed look alike? No, the apple seed is smaller. The peach seed is big, hard and has ridges on it.

Do all seeds look alike? No God made each kind of seed to look different from other kinds of seeds.

When God made the earth, He put the seed of animals, birds, fish, fruits, and plants for every kind of thing to have its own babies and grow again from its kind of seed in it.

Why do you think God put seeds inside of the things He made? (Listen to Responses) God planned for everything to have babies and grow again from the kind of seed He put in it. God did not have to make the same things over again because its seed would grow it again.

Did you know that God put the seed inside of the first man Adam for all people to be born from Adam?

Yes, and you and all people, your mommy, daddy, and everyone was born from the seed that God put in Adam.
Let's see who can answer this question the quickest!
What is the name of the man that God put the seed inside of for all people to be born from?
(Listen to Responses)

Adam!

Parent/Teacher Script, (continued):

That's right! All people were born from the seed in Adam.
We are going to have a SEED CONTEST.
You are each getting a paper plate.
(Distribute paper plates)

Draw one picture of a different fruit on each section of the plate.
Only draw a fruit that you have seen a seed inside of it.
You can take your plate home to find a seed from every fruit that you drew.
Glue the seed of that fruit next to the picture you drew.
Everyone who brings their plate back with the seeds WINS.

WHEN CHILDREN RETURN THEIR PLATES:
(Give everyone that brings their plate back with any seeds a ribbon or a sticker.)

ASK THESE TWO QUESTIONS AGAIN:
1) Why do you think God put seeds inside of the things He made?
   (Listen to Responses)

   God planned for everything to have babies and grow again from the kind of seed He put in it. God did not have to make the same things over again because its seed would grow.

2) What is the name of the man that God put the seed inside of for all people to be born from?
   (Listen to Responses)

   Adam! All people were born from the seed in Adam.

Additional Activity:
Plant seeds, water as needed, and place the planted seeds in an area where they can get appropriate amount of sunlight to grow.

Outcome: Children can see that a plant can grow again from its seed.

Scriptures:
Genesis 1:11-12, 1:20-22, 1:24-25, 1:26-30

FOLLOW UP ACTIVITY
DO YOU KNOW HOW MUCH FATHER LOVES YOU?

Objectives to be Understood: God, your heavenly Father loves you with an everlasting love.

Activity: To make a tiny baby (from a clothes pin) to represent themselves and role-play how God held them in His hand.

Materials: Clothes pins, glue, markers, yarn (for hair colors of black, brown, red, yellow), scissors (to cut yarn in one and two inch pieces) and small pieces of cloth (wide enough to wrap around clothes pin)

Parent/Teacher Script:
Did you know that God, your Father, loves you? Listen to a few
things He said about you in His Word that is written in the Holy Bible.
- His eyes saw you before you were formed in your mommy's belly.
- He covered you (protected you) when you were in your mommy's belly.
- All of the days of your life were meant for Him.
- He wrote about you in His book before you were born.
- He planned for you to succeed before you were born.
- He thinks about you.
- You are so valuable to Him that He came Himself, as Jesus, to rescue you from sin and death.
- God has ministering angels sent to you.
- He sings over you!
- He knows how many hairs you have on your head.
- He sent Holy Spirit to live in you, His child, who chose to believe and receive Him so that you could be one with Him and Jesus.

What are some ways we could let our heavenly Father know we love Him.
(Listen to responses)

(To begin activity: Place materials out where child can reach)

P.A.C.E.
www.ABC-Jesus.com
© All Rights Reserved

Activity:
1) We are going to make a baby from a clothes pin and pretend it's you.
2) You can draw a face on it with a marker.
3) You can glue yarn on its head for hair.
4) You can wrap your baby with some cloth.
5) After you finish:
    a. You can sing over your baby like God sings over you.
    b. You can count its hair.
    c. You can rock your baby in your hand and sing like God sings over you.

Scriptures:
Psalm 139:13-17; Hebrews 1:14; Zephaniah 3:17; Matthew 10:30; Romans 8:11; Romans 5:8; Jeremiah 29:11; Ephesians 1:4-5; John 17:21

THE FALL OF MAN
(Read Book 2)

PARENT LETTER 2

Dear Parents,

We ask that you help your child to understand these two truths from lesson 2 in preparation for next week's lesson about "JESUS" and being born again as a child of God.
(John 3:5-6; John 17:17)

God made us in three parts: spirit, soul and body.

Ask your child to answer Mystery Question # 1.
What has three parts but is one person?

Answer: You! You are one person with three parts.
1) You are a spirit like heavenly Father.

2) God made you a living soul which is your mind and your feelings.

3) You have a body. Your spirit and soul live in your body.
    (John 4:24; I Thessalonians 5:23; Hebrews 4:12)

God made us with the ability to choose.

Ask your child to answer Mystery Question # 2.
Why do you think God lets everyone choose?

Answer: God wants everyone to freely choose His love and believe Him from their heart. God does not force anyone to choose Him. God lets you choose who you will serve. Every choice you make is either good and on God's side; OR it is bad and on the devil's side.
(Deuteronomy 30:19)

One of the Follow Up Activities is entitled "Which Kingdom Do You Choose?" When your child completes it, ask about the picture of the kingdom they made. Ask why they chose that kingdom. Post your child's picture somewhere in your home where they can see it. Talk to your child about kingdoms. Let them know that kingdoms are ruled by kings who make laws for the people in the kingdom. One of the laws of God is whoever you choose to believe and obey is who rules over you, either God or the devil.
(Romans 6:16)

We pray that hearts are prepared to make the right choice and receive the true love of God from our Father in heaven!
(John 3:5-7; John 3:16-17; Romans 10:9-13)

Sincerely in Christ,

Your Child's Teacher
Contact information: _____

FOLLOW UP ACTIVITIES

FOLLOW-UP ACTIVITY
I CHOOSE GOD!

Objectives to be Understood: For children and adults to sing together this fun and happy song about choosing God!

Tune: Sing to the tune of London Bridge is Falling Down.

I choose God because God loves me.
God loves me.
God loves me.
I choose God because God loves me.
God loves me all day long.

With God's love I choose to sing.
Choose to sing.
Choose to sing.
With God's love I choose to sing.
I sing a happy song.

FOLLOW-UP ACTIVITY
PRAYING TO FATHER

Objectives to be Understood:
1. For children to know why it is important to choose to listen and obey God;
2. To pray in their own words to Father, and;
3. That God has told us to pray for certain things.

Materials: None

Parent/Teacher Script:
Your Father in heaven loves you! God's kingdom is full of love. In God's kingdom He thinks about you and has made good plans for you. The devil's kingdom is full of hate. The devil wants to hurt you.

Father told Jesus to tell you to pray for certain things. One thing Father told you to pray and ask Him is for His kingdom to come to earth. Why do you think Father wants His kingdom on earth, instead of the devil's kingdom? (Listen to Answers) Father wants everyone to have His love. Father does not want anyone to be hurt by listening to the devil. So God, your heavenly Father wants you to pray and ask Him for His Kingdom to come to earth. When you choose to obey Father and pray for what He told you, then He can show you His good Kingdom of love.

The good angels in heaven chose to believe and obey Father because they knew God is good and He loves them. Everything that God tells you to do is always for your good. Father also asked you to pray that His will be done on earth, just like it is in heaven. Can you think of any good thing that God may want you to do on earth, like it is in heaven? *(Listen to Answers)*

In heaven, God's Kingdom is full of love! Everyone loves heavenly Father and all the other people in heaven. Your Father wants you to also love Him and other people on earth. But sometimes a person might act mean and NOT show love like in God's Kingdom. That's why Father told you to pray. God wants you to pray and ask Him to help the person to know His love.

When you pray and ask Father for His kingdom to come and for His will to be done on earth just like it is in heaven, YOU ARE OBEYING HIM!

Why do you think it is important to listen and obey God? *(Listen to Answers)* When you listen and obey God, it shows Him that you love Him.

Think of someone who needs God's Kingdom of love and let's pray for them. You can use your own words and pray it your own way. Father will hear you and understand you no matter how you say it. You can talk to Father about everything. You can pray now and anytime you choose. Remember to always thank Him! God loves you and will hear your prayer. Let's pray softly.

Scriptures:
Jeremiah 29:11-13; Matthew 6:10; Matthew 5:43-45; John 14:15; I Thessalonians 5:16-18; I John 5:14-15

FOLLOW UP ACTIVITY
SPIRIT, SOUL, AND BODY

Objectives to be Understood:
1) God made you a living soul;
2) the living part of you is your spirit;
3) your spirit and soul live in your body;
4) your spirit and soul does not die, but lives forever with whomever you chose to believe, either God or the devil.

Materials: one (1) pre-made puppet to use with the Parent/Teacher Script below:
TO MAKE PUPPETS WITH CHILDREN: socks or paper bags (enough for each child), glue, colored pencils, colored markers, crayons, assorted colors of yarn, felt, scissors, buttons, etc.

Parent/Teacher Script:
God is a Spirit. A spirit is like the wind and your breath. Wind is real but you can't see it. Blow your breath onto your hand. (Encourage children to blow on their hand) You can feel your breath and know that it is real, but you cannot see it. Since God is a Spirit and He made you to look like Him and to be like Him, where do you think He put your spirit?
(Listen to responses)

God put your spirit inside of your body. Your body is on the outside of you like a house and you can see it and touch it. But your spirit and soul live inside of your body. Your soul is your mind, your will and your feelings. Your soul and your spirit are the real you.

Your spirit gives life to your body. Did you know that if your spirit were not in your body it would die? It is sort of like this puppet.
(Hold up a puppet)

Let's pretend that this puppet is my body. And let's pretend that my hand is my spirit. *(Insert your hand into the puppet and make it move)* When my hand is in the puppet I can choose how I want it to move and what I want it to say. *(Move puppet around, and say words to the children like,* Hi Boys and girls! My name is ….)

But when my spirit comes out of my body like my hand out of the puppet, it cannot move or do anything. *(Remove your hand from inside puppet)* When there is nothing with life inside the puppet to make it move, the puppet cannot move. *(Drop the puppet)* When your spirit is not in your body, your body is dead. Your spirit is what gives life to your body. Have you ever seen someone or something that has died? *(Listen to responses)* Their body is dead but the real person which is their spirit and soul is still alive.
Their spirit and soul left their body to go and live forever with whoever they chose to believe when they were in their body. If they believed Jesus when their spirit was in their body, their spirit and soul will go home to heaven to be with Father and Jesus forever. Their spirit and

Parent/Teacher Script, (continued)**:**

soul will not die, but will pass from life on earth to life in heaven. But if they believed the lies of the devil when their spirit was in their body, then their soul will not go to heaven but with the devil and his demons forever. Do you understand? Whoever you choose to believe is who rules over you, either God or the devil.

Answer these questions:
Which part of you will live forever and is the real you?
Is it your body?
Or is it your spirit and your soul?
Your spirit and soul will live forever and is the real you!
We are going to make a puppet. Then we can have fun making our puppets move and talk when we have our hands in them—like how our spirit give life to our body.

Making Puppets Instructions:

1) Decide the type of puppets to make, such as sock puppets, paper bag puppets, paper plate puppets, etc.
2) Provide the materials for children to decorate the faces of their puppets with eyes, nose, mouth, hair or however they want to decorate their puppets.

Scriptures:
I Thessalonians 5:23; John 3:8; John 4:24; John 6:63; James 2:26; Matthew 10:28;
I John 5:11-13; Revelation 20:11-15

FOLLOW UP ACTIVITY
WHICH KINGDOM DO YOU CHOOSE?

Objectives to be Understood:
1) There is a very bad devil on the earth, and
2) There are two kingdoms operating on earth, the kingdom of God and the kingdom of the devil, and everyone must choose which kingdom they will serve.

Materials: Assorted items such as construction or plain paper, colored pencils, colored markers, crayons, confetti stars, stickers, scissors, glue, etc.

Parent/Teacher Script:
Do you remember who was kicked out of heaven?
(Listen to responses)

The devil and his bad angels were kicked out of heaven.
Why were they kicked out of heaven?
(Listen to responses)

The bad angels wanted to take over heaven so they fought with God's good angels.
Is the devil and his bad angels still in heaven or is the devil on the earth?
(Listen to responses)

The devil and his bad angels are on the earth.
Do you remember who Adam and Eve obeyed and made the leader of the earth?
(Listen to responses)

The devil! When Adam and Eve believed the devil he set up a spirit kingdom on the earth. You cannot see a spirit kingdom with your eyes. Just like you cannot see the wind but you can feel it. In the devil's kingdom he tells lies to people to try to make them think and do bad things. He wants to steal, kill and destroy people in a very bad place called hell. The devil wants to trick you so that you will believe and choose him. The devil's kingdom is dark, ugly and full of hate. Let's say BOO to the devil's ugly kingdom!
(Everyone shout BOO!)

God, your heavenly Father has a Kingdom! God's Kingdom is full of light and love!
Did you know that God is Love? (Listen to responses)
God is TRUE Love! When you think of God's kind of love what comes to your mind?
(Listen to responses)

God's Kingdom has rainbows and God's Kingdom is fun! No one is sick and no one hurts anyone. God's Kingdom is full of light and He has many good things just for you. God wants you to choose His Kingdom, but He will NOT make you choose Him. Let's cheer and say YAY to God's beautiful Kingdom of Love!
(Everyone shout YAY!)
Instructions:

Give each child paper, pencils, etc. and instruct the children to draw and decorate one picture of the kingdom they choose.

After each child has drawn and decorated their kingdom, ASK: "would you like to show which kingdom you chose?" *When the child shows the kingdom they chose,* ASK: "why did you choose that kingdom?"

<u>Note</u>: If a child chooses the kingdom of darkness, do not condemn them. The child simply has a lack of understanding. Therefore when you are alone, pray for the child that God would remove spiritual blinders, according to 2 Cor. 3:13-17. Then later reread and discuss Story Lesson 2 with the children.

Scriptures:
Isaiah 14:12; Revelation 12:9; Genesis 3:6; Matthew 4:8-9, 4:17; 2 Corinthians 4:18; 10:3-6; Joshua 24:15

FOLLOW UP ACTIVITY
TELL ME SOMETHING GOOD!

Objectives to be Understood: For children to practice thinking and speaking good things like Father instructed us.

Materials: Paper and pen or pencil

Number of Participants: Two or more

Instructions:
Choose one note taker to write down all the good things said about each person.
One person is chosen to begin the activity by saying, Tell Me Something Good!

Each person takes a turn thinking and saying one **different** good thing (from their heart) about the person who said, Tell Me Something Good!
(Different means to say something that someone else has not said)

When everyone has had a turn saying a **different** good thing about the first person, it's the next person's turn to say, Tell Me Something Good!

Then each person takes a turn thinking and saying one **different** good thing about the second person who said, Tell Me Something Good!

If a person cannot think of a **different** good thing, they can say Pass.
The activity continues repeating instructions 1-6 with each person thinking and saying one different good thing about each person when it is their turn.
Give each person their list of good things after the game ends.

Activity Variations:
Say one different good thing about:
God, your heavenly Father!
Something that happened today!
The local police!
Rain!
The town you are in!
Your parents!

Scriptures:
Philippians 4:8; Romans 12:10; Romans 13:8; Romans 14:19

FOLLOW UP ACTIVITY
GOD CANNOT LIE!

Objectives to be Understood:
1) the devil is the father of lies and God speaks only truth and He cannot lie.
2) to know the difference between God's words of truth and a lie.

Materials: One copy for each child of The Truth (happy face) and A Lie (sad face); Scissors; Instructions; The Truth or A Lie Statements.

Parent/Teacher Script:
When Adam and Eve were in the Garden of Eden they did not believe their Father's words. The Words that Father said to Adam and Eve was the truth. Father always tells the truth! God, our Father cannot lie. But the devil always tells lies! The devil is the father of lies. Did you know that on the day Adam and Eve listened to the lies of the devil and disobeyed their Father, that God already knew they had disobeyed Him? *(Listen to Responses)* Yes, Father knows all things. But He gives everyone the right to choose who they will believe and obey.

Have you ever done something wrong that your parents or someone else told you NOT to do?
(Listen to Answers)

How would you feel if you got caught doing something wrong?
(Listen to Answers)

How do you think Adam felt when he heard his Father walking towards him after he disobeyed Him?
(Listen to Answers)

Adam said he hid because he was afraid.
Why do you think Adam was afraid of his Father?
(Listen to Answers)

Why do you think Adam lied and tried to put all of the blame on Eve?
(Listen to Answers)

Have you ever said something that was NOT true?
(Listen to Answers)

When you let your tongue say something that is not true, you are telling a lie. God loves you, but He hates when you let your tongue tell a lie. When you tell a lie, are you listening to God or the devil?
(Listen to Answers)

When you tell a lie you are listening to the devil. The devil invented lies.

Parent/Teacher Script, (continued):

Let's do a fun activity called The Truth or A Lie to practice knowing the difference between the truth of what our Father has said, and a lie.

TRUTH OR LIE ACTIVITY

Parent/Teacher Script: Every Word that God says is TRUE because God can not lie. This means that God's Word is THE TRUTH. It is important to know what God has said so that you will know the difference between THE TRUTH, and something that is not true, which is A LIE. Before we begin, let's see if you remember! Let's say it together. God's Word is
(pause)

THE TRUTH! Let's say it again. God's Word is
(pause)

THE TRUTH! Let's say it one more time. God's Word is *(pause)* THE TRUTH! That's right! God's Word is THE TRUTH and A LIE is not true!

Instructions:
- Copy and cut out along the dotted line one (The Truth) happy face, and one (A Lie) sad face for each child.
- Instruct the children to place the two pictures in front of themselves so they can see the happy and sad faces.
- Ask the children to listen carefully to the words you will read to them.
- Tell the children to Hold up the Happy Face if they think the Words you read were from God and THE TRUTH.
- Or, hold up the Sad Face if they think the words are NOT true, but A LIE from the devil.
- Choose one TRUTH or LIE Statement and read it aloud to the children.
- Whichever statement is read, the truth or the lie, the next statement read should be its counterpart, right next to it.
- After each child shows the face they chose, ask, why did you choose that face? *(Encourage conversation to promote understanding)*

THE TRUTH OR A LIE STATEMENTS

A LIE	THE TRUTH
You are not special to God!	God said, "I have called you by your name. You are mine!" (You are special to God.) Isaiah 43:1
God will not forgive you for that bad thing you did!	God said if you tell Him what you did, He will forgive you! I John 1:9
God hates you!	God proved that He loves you when He said He would send His Son Jesus to save you! (God loves you!) John 3:16; I John 3:1; John 17:23
You can tell a lie!	God hates when anyone lets their tongue tell a lie. Proverbs 6:16-19
God will never answer your prayer!	God said when you pray for the good things that He wants for you, He answers your prayer! I John 5:14-15

Cut along dotted line → ------------------------------

THE TRUTH

John 17:17

Cut along dotted line → ------------------------------

A LIE

John 8:44

Cut along dotted line → ------------------------------

Scriptures:
Genesis 2:17; Genesis 3:4-5; John 8:44; John17:17; Titus 1:2; Psalm 89:34; Isaiah 55:11; Numbers 23:19; Luke 21:33; Proverbs 6:16-19

FOLLOW UP ACTIVITY
CHOOSE!

Objectives to be Understood: For children to understand that God wants you to choose to listen to His Words and choose to obey Him and your parents in the Lord.

Number of participants: 2 or more

Materials: 24 CHOICE cards; Score Sheet; scissors, pencil

Parent/Teacher Script:
God's Word says that when you love Him, you will choose to obey Him. He also tells you to obey your parents in the Lord. You show your parents that you love them when you choose to obey them also. God, your Father knows that if you choose to not listen to your parents on earth that you will not listen to Him. We are going to play a fun activity to help you remember that love chooses to listen and obey God.

Instructions:
Run a copy of the Score Sheet and CHOICE cards. Cut out the 24 CHOICE cards.
The parent/teacher is the scorekeeper. The scorekeeper writes the scores of each player and gives each player their total score at the end of the activity.
Mix the cards. Give each player one CHOICE card. Place the remaining cards in a stack. Instruct each player to not let anyone see his or her card. If a player cannot read, they can ask the parent/teacher to read the words on their card to them.
Each player gets a turn one at a time to choose to do one thing on his or her card.
The first player reads their card to themselves.
The first player chooses to do one of the things on the card.
The other players try to guess what the first player chose to do.
Place used cards in a separate pile.

The activity continues repeating instructions 3 – 9 until everyone has had a turn.

TO END THE ACTIVITY: It is IMPORTANT TO SAY the Parent/Teacher script below!
Parent/Teacher Script: (Say to all players *after* CHOICE Game ends)
"You made a choice to either OBEY what was on the card or DO NOTHING that was on the card. The same way you chose to obey or not obey the words on the card, you also choose whether you will listen and obey God. Everything you do is a choice!

Scriptures:
Joshua 24:15; Ephesians 6:1-3; John 14:23; I John 5:2-3

CHOICE CARDS

CHOOSE 1 Woof like a dog. 2 points OR Hug someone. 5 points OR Do Nothing. 0 points	**CHOOSE 1** Cock a Doodle Doo like a rooster. 2 points OR Tell someone you like them. 5 points OR Do Nothing. 0 points
CHOOSE 1 Moo like a cow. 2 points OR Hug someone. 5 points OR Do Nothing. 0 points	**CHOOSE 1** Hop like a rabbit. 2 points OR Tell someone you like them. 5 points OR Do Nothing. 0 points
CHOOSE 1 Cluck like a chicken. 2 points OR Hug someone. 5 points OR Do Nothing. 0 points	**CHOOSE 1** BAAA like a Sheep. 2 points OR Tell someone you like them. 5 points OR Do Nothing. 0 points
CHOOSE 1 Croak like a Frog. 2 points OR Hug someone. 5 points OR Do Nothing. 0 points	**CHOOSE 1** Growl like a bear. 2 points OR Tell someone you like them. 5 points OR Do Nothing. 0 points
CHOOSE 1 He Haw like a Donkey. 2 points OR Hug someone. 5 points OR Do Nothing. 0 points	**CHOOSE 1** Howl like a Wolf. 2 points OR Tell someone you like them. 5 points OR Do Nothing. 0 points
CHOOSE 1 Laugh like a Hyena. 2 points OR Hug someone. 5 points OR Do Nothing. 0 points	**CHOOSE 1** Chatter like a Squirrel. 2 points OR Tell someone you like them. 5 points OR Do Nothing. 0 points

CHOICE CARDS

CHOOSE 1 Meow like a cat. 2 points OR Hug someone. 5 points OR Do Nothing. 0 points	**CHOOSE 1** Oink like a pig. 2 points OR Tell someone you like them. 5 points OR Do Nothing. 0 points
CHOOSE 1 Caw like a crow. 2 points OR Hug someone. 5 points OR Do Nothing. 0 points	**CHOOSE 1** Naa like a horse. 2 points OR Tell someone you like them. 5 points OR Do Nothing. 0 points
CHOOSE 1 Hoot like an owl. 2 points OR Hug someone. 5 points OR Do Nothing. 0 points	**CHOOSE 1** Buzz like a Bee. 2 points OR Tell someone you like them. 5 points OR Do Nothing. 0 points
CHOOSE 1 Roar like a Lion. 2 points OR Hug someone. 5 points OR Do Nothing. 0 points	**CHOOSE 1** Squeak like a Mouse. 2 points OR Tell someone you like them. 5 points OR Do Nothing. 0 points
CHOOSE 1 Gobble like a Turkey. 2 points OR Hug someone. 5 points OR Do Nothing. 0 points	**CHOOSE 1** Cry like a Baby. 2 points OR Tell someone you like them. 5 points OR Do Nothing. 0 points
CHOOSE 1 Chirp like a Cricket. 2 points OR Hug someone. 5 points OR Do Nothing. 0 points	**CHOOSE 1** Flap your arms like the wings of a bird. 2 points OR Tell someone you like them. 5 points OR Do Nothing. 0 points

CHOICE SCORE SHEET

Names	Scores	Scores	Scores	Total Score
1.				
2.				
3.				
4.				
5.				
6.				

Names	Scores	Scores	Scores	Total Score
1.				
2.				
3.				
4.				
5.				
6.				

FOLLOW UP ACTIVITY
THE LAWS OF THE KINGDOM!

Objectives to be Understood:
    1) God made laws and rules for your good,
    2) God will not break His laws, and
    3) you can help others be safe when you obey God's good rules.

Number of participants: four or more

Materials: None

Parent/Teacher Script:
God made good laws. Laws are rules. Have you ever played a game?

When you play a game the game has rules. The rules help you to know how to play the game so that you can have fun playing with friends. But if there were no rules everyone would do something different and you or your friends could get hurt.

God's made good laws and rules for the earth and you to obey. God's laws keep things in order so people do not get hurt. God's laws are in the spirit. You cannot see all of God's laws, but we can tell His laws are here. Listen to some of the good laws God has made for you.

God made the law of gravity. Gravity is what keeps you and everything on the earth from floating away into space. God made the law of sin and death. The law of sin and death is that anyone who sins must die. God also made the law of faith which is greater than the law of sin and death. Faith is when you believe the things God has said, He will do it. God's Word is a promise and He cannot lie. God does not break His promises or His laws.

God wants you to know He loves you so He made laws and rules to keep you safe and for you to believe Him. Let's play a game without rules and a game with rules so you can see how rules and laws help us. Let's play Simon Says without rules.
(Let the children try to play Simon Says without rules.)

Remind the children that they CANNOT follow rules because there are no rules.

If someone tries to make rules, remind them there are no laws or rules.

After a few minutes, call everyone back together.

Parent/Teacher Script, (continued)**:**

With no rules, we cannot decide who will be the leader to tell us what Simon wants us to do or not do. Everyone might decide to be the leader and that would be confusing. It's hard to play with no rules.

Let's play a game with rules this time. Our game is called God Says. The rules are the same as Simon Says only instead of saying Simon Says, you say God Says.

The players are only to do what God says. If someone does something and the leader did not say that God says to do it, that person is out of the game.

Everyone line up against the wall
(or in a designated area).

Instructions
1. Choose a leader to call out the instructions of what to do by saying things such as, God Says, take one small step. (Everyone should take one small step because they are following the laws or rules of the game)
2. If the leader calls out an instruction without saying God Says, and a person does it, that person is out of the game.
3. The last person playing is the winner.

After playing the game, Remind children how much easier it was to play the game with rules to follow. God knew that people would need rules and laws so God made laws to keep us safe.

Scriptures:
Romans 3:27-28; Romans 7:14; Romans 8:2; Romans 10:17

FOLLOW UP ACTIVITY
WHAT DID GOD SAY? LESSON 2

Objectives to be Understood: For children to know:
1) God made you to be like Him;
2) God's Word is alive and true;
3) God's Word is like a sword;
4) God's Word has the power of life in it, and;
5) To say what God has said.

ACTIVITY: Children will write in their books the Scriptures/Words God Said.
IMPORTANT NOTE: This activity is included in each of our 6 lessons with a different scripture in each lesson for children to receive into their hearts.

MATERIALS: Pencils; Markers; Pre-made book template or purchased notebooks
(see Preparation below)

Preparation: To MAKE A BOOK
Pre-make book templates for each child by folding two sheets of paper in half and stapling (two staples on the folded side so pages open like a book); OR purchase lined notebooks.

Write out and post (where children can easily see) the following scripture:

TRUE LOVE IS GOD'S LOVE FOR US, NOT OUR LOVE FOR GOD.
HE SENT HIS SON AS THE WAY TO TAKE AWAY OUR SINS!
1 John 4:10

REVIEW:
What makes the Bible different from other books?
(Listen to Responses)

The difference is the Bible is full of God's Words that are ALIVE and TRUE.
God's living words have POWER in them and can change things when you believe what God has said.

Did God make everything to be good or evil?

God made everything to be good and come alive by His Word. God's Word is written in the Bible. This is why it is very important that you learn the things that God has said in the Bible.

Different writers wrote what God told them to write in the Bible. What are the Words in the Bible called? The Words in the Bible are called scriptures.

What are the different parts of the Bible called? The different parts of the Bible are called books. The scripture or words that we will learn today can be found in the book of 1st John the fourth chapter and the 10th verse. I John 4:10
(Show children 1 John 4:10 in Bible)

The Bible has stories about God, and people. Some people believed God and others did not believe Him. The Bible is God's Word written to us.

TO KNOW GOD'S WORD

First, you must LET YOUR EARS HEAR GOD'S WORD AND BELIEVE IT.
Second, LET YOUR MOUTH SAY THE WORDS THAT GOD HAS SAID.
Third, Tell your mind to THINK ABOUT WHAT GOD HAS SAID.
When you think about what God has said, HIS WORD GOES INSIDE YOUR HEART. And your heart will help you love like God.

If you would like God, your heavenly Father to help you to know Him and the Words He has said, you can pray and say these words after me, or you can pray to God in your own words. Ready. Let's pray!

PRAYER

Father,
(Pause for Children to Repeat)
I want to know You
(Pause)
Will you help me?
(Pause)
I want to hear and believe You
(Pause)
Will You teach me to say
(Pause)
what You have said every day?
(Pause)
Thank You Father!
(Pause)
Will you help me
(Pause)
to think about Your Word?
(Pause)
Thank You Father!
(Pause)
Will You let Your Word
(Pause)
change my heart
(Pause)
so I will love like You?
(Pause)
Thank You for hearing me
(Pause)
and answering my prayer!
(Pause)
I love You!
(Pause)
Amen.

LEARNING SCRIPTURES FOR OUR BOOKS

PARENT/TEACHER SCRIPT:
Does anyone have something good to tell us that God did for you from His Word?
(Listen to the testimonies of the children)

We are going to add a new scripture to our What Did God Say books?
(Show children the Lesson 2 Scripture and let children know these are some Words God said)

Our new scripture is: "True love is God's love for us, not our love for God. He sent His Son as the way to take away our sins."

What do you think God means when He said, "True love is God's love for us, not our love for God. He sent His Son as the way to take away our sins"?
(Listen to Responses)

Adam and Eve sinned when they did not believe their Father's Words and disobeyed Him. After Adam and Eve sinned, almost everyone began to sin, but God never stopped loving Adam, Eve, and all people. God promised to send His Son to take away our sins.
Why do you think God promised to send His Son Jesus?
(Listen to Responses)

God's love is a true agape love. He wants everyone to know His awesome heavenly love. He does not want anyone to be hurt by choosing not to believe His love for you. So Father said He would send His Son to die in your place, and take away all sins so you could live and choose to know Him. This is why He said, "True love is God's love for us, not our love for God." For when we were sinning, He loved us and promised to send His Son Jesus to take away our sins. God's love is big and true.

Let's say this scripture boldly together.

True love
(children repeat)
is God's love for us,
(children repeat)
not our love for God.
(children repeat)
He sent His Son
(children repeat)
as the way
(children repeat)
to take away our sins.
Let's say it again!
(Repeat Scripture)

P.A.C.E.
www.ABC-Jesus.com
© All Rights Reserved

Parent/Teacher Script, (continued)**:**

Have you ever had someone to tell you they love you?
(Listen to responses)

Your Father in heaven loves you with a love that is not like the love on earth. His love is called agape love. Agape love is a heavenly amazing love.
Repeat after me!
God loves me
(children repeat)
and He sent His Son Jesus
(children repeat)
to take away my sins.
Did you know that God's love is true?
(Listen to responses)

It is so true that the more you say what God has said, the power in God's words will go into your heart to live. And you will know the truth. And the truth is God loves you!

Let's say this scripture boldly together again.

True love
(children repeat)
is God's love for us,
(children repeat)
not our love for God.
(children repeat)
He sent His Son
(children repeat)
as the way
(children repeat)
to take away our sins.
Let's say it again!
(Repeat Scripture)

Ask children to take out their books.
(CHILDREN WHO DID NOT BRING THEIR NOTE BOOKS, let them write their scripture on paper. Tell them to put it in their book when they get home.) (Provide notebooks for new children or make new book templates for this lesson.)

Write God's Words in your book.
Everyday read your book. Declare and say God's Words so your ears can Hear His Words!
Every day pay attention and watch God do what He said because you believed Him, and you

said what He said. When you see God do what He said, write or draw a picture in your book about the good things God did for you.
And come tell us about it.
(If children are using notebooks, remind them to bring them back so they can continue to write more Words that God said in it.)

Let's Sing these Words God Said:
(Sing to the tune of "If you're happy and you know it")

**True love is God's love for us. Not our love for God!
True love is God's love for us. Not our love for God!
He sent His Son to take away our sins.
True love is God's love for us.**
(Repeat Several Times)

SONG: GOD LOVES ME!
(Sung to the tune of Barney Song)
(Do motions to Song)
YOU LOVE ME!
(Point upward, then to self)
I LOVE YOU!
(Point to self and upward)
YOU MAKE MY HEART GO PITTER-PAT!
(Point up, touch heart, Clap hands as you say pitter-pat)
YOU LOVED ME FIRST
(Point upward, then to self)
AND I LOVE YOU BACK!
(Kiss your hands and blow kisses up to Father)
YOU MAKE MY HEART GO PITTER-PAT!
(Point up, touch your heart, then clap hands as you say pitter-pat)
I LOVE YOU FATHER!
(Lift both hands up and SHOUT)

Scriptures:
I John 4:10; I Corinthians 13:8; John 3:16; 2 John 1:6

JESUS
(Read Book 3)

PARENT LETTER 3

Dear Parents;
Today our lesson offered your child the choice to believe Jesus died for their sins, become a child of God, and receive Father's gifts of Holy Spirit and speaking in tongues. See the box checked below regarding your child's decision.

- ☐ Yes, your child chose to believe Jesus and become a child of God today!
- ☐ Yes, your child received Father's gift of Holy Spirit!
- ☐ Yes, your child spoke with the gift of tongues!
- ☐ Your child already knew Jesus as their Lord and Savior!
- ☐ Your child participated in Holy Communion.
- ☐ Your child would benefit from more information about:_____

If today your child accepted what Jesus did for us all, the Word of God says your child was saved. (Romans 10:9-10; Acts 2:21) To be saved means that your child's life was redeemed or saved from sin and death by Jesus. (Romans 3:23-26; 6:9-12) Jesus died for everyone to fulfill God's law that says the penalty or wages of sin is death. (Romans 6:23) Jesus defeated the devil and took the keys of death and hell. (Revelation 1:18) God raised Jesus from the dead. (Romans 6:4) In choosing to believe Jesus, the Word of God says your child was given eternal life and restored to a right relationship with God as their eternal Father.
(John 17:2-3; Romans 5:9-11; 8:14-16)

Therefore to foster a clear understanding of why we needed a Savior and what Jesus did for us, we encourage you to read this story of JESUS aloud a minimum of three to six times and let your child retell parts they know. Talk about what happened to Jesus in the story, how Jesus must have felt, and how much heavenly Father must love you to send Jesus to suffer and die in your place.

As you review the story, remind your child that God gave us a special language to speak directly to Him from our spirit. (I Corinthians 14:2) And s/he can pray to Father in the special language of tongues whenever they chose.

Let your child know that when they chose to be born again as a child of God it was the greatest and best choice they could ever make on earth.
(Galatians 3:26-29; Romans 8:16-18)

If your child received Jesus today, this is an important day in their life and should be remembered, so we celebrate with you and your child by giving them a certificate of this special day. We have also sent you some celebration ideas.

Water Baptism: Please plan for a water baptism for your child. (Acts 10:47) Talk with him/her about water baptism and how it represents what happened to them when they received Jesus.

P.A.C.E.
www.ABC-Jesus.com
© All Rights Reserved

(Acts 2:38) Explain that the going down into the water shows their belief that Jesus died for them, that their sins have been washed away and buried. (Acts 22:16; Romans 6:3-4) Coming out of the water shows that they have been raised up as a new creation in Christ Jesus. *(Galatians 3:27; 2 Corinthians 5:17)*

Parents, we pray for you.

Heavenly Father,
We ask that You remind (*insert your name*) that You are the God of all mercy, grace and agape love, and that (*insert your name*) can come to You as Father anytime to receive Your help and guidance to raise up her/his child/ren Your way. We ask You Father to give (*insert your name*) wisdom to guide these child/ren that You placed in *her/his* care to *be* and *do* all that You spoke into them and planned for them before the foundations of the earth. We humbly ask in Jesus Name that You bless (*insert your name*) and *her/his* child/ren to live and grow fully in Your love and care all the days of their life! Amen.

Sincerely in Christ,

Your Child's Teacher
Contact information: _____

FOLLOW UP ACTIVITIES

FOLLOW UP ACTIVITY
I'M A CHILD OF GOD!   LET'S CELEBRATE!

Objectives to be Understood: For children to understand the day they were "Born Again" is a special and important day to remember.

Activity: Plan a party to celebrate the day the child was Born Again as a child of Father.

Materials: Paper, markers, tape (or something to write on like a chalk board); Party items such as, streamers, Happy Birthday banner, balloons, party hats, snack items such as juice, cake, cookies, etc.

Parent/Teacher Script: If you believed Jesus and received Holy Spirit into your heart, you have two birthdays. Your first birthday was when you were born on earth from God in Adam through your parents. Your second birthday was when you were "Born Again" by the Spirit of God in Jesus as a child of God, your heavenly Father.

Tell children we will have a party to celebrate the day you were "Born Again" as a child of God. What are some things you would like to do to thank your heavenly Father and Jesus and celebrate your "Born Again" second birthday?
(Listen to the responses and write down the things you agree upon)

Some ideas:
Plan fun games! Ask the children: What are some games you would like to play?
Plan time to praise, dance and thank God.
Plan to sing the Happy Birthday song.
Plan to make a birthday card to give to each other.
Give children their certificate of "The Day I Believed In Jesus!"
Party and have fun celebrating the child's new life in Christ Jesus!

Scriptures:
John 3:5-7; 2 Corinthians 5:17

CERTIFICATE

OF
THE DAY I BELIEVED IN JESUS

**AND WAS BORN-AGAIN
AS A CHILD OF HEAVENLY FATHER!**

_____
My Signature

_____
Date

FOLLOW UP ACTIVITY
JESUS OUR SUPER HERO!

Objectives to be Understood:
1) there is no one greater than heavenly Father and our Super Hero Jesus; and
2) you can practice Super Love everyday by showing loving kindness to others from your heart.

Activity: Children will:
1) picture read to retell Story Lesson 3, "JESUS," answer questions, and;
2) make a Super Love T-shirt.

Materials: Story Lesson 3, "JESUS" book; white T-shirts with no writing or art on them; colored and lead pencils; paper; erasers; fabric markers

Instructions:
Show the picture pages from Story Lesson 3, "JESUS," and encourage the children to retell the story from the pictures. (End the story at the page that shows Jesus caught up to heaven to be with His Father.)

Tell the children: Jesus is the GREATEST Super Hero ever!

Ask the children: What do you think Jesus did to be the greatest Super Hero ever? *(Listen to the Responses of the children)* Jesus showed love to people. He healed the sick. He made the devil stop bothering people. He made dead people come back to life. And Jesus died for you, me and everyone in the world!

Ask: Why do you think Jesus died for us? *(Listen to the Responses of the children)* Jesus died in our place so all people could know Father's love.

Tell the children: Jesus is greater than any make-believe hero that you may see on television or read about in a book. Jesus is greater than the make-believe batman. Greater than the make-believe superman. Greater than any make-believe hero. No one can do what Jesus has done! Jesus is the only one who went to hell for you, beat the devil, and was raised from hell by Father's Holy Spirit so everyone could be saved from sin and death!

Let's sing this new song about Jesus.

(To the tune of *Late last night when we were all in bed Old Lady Leary*)

(Sing at least two times for children to learn words and motions)
**Jesus my Super Hero He's always there for me!
The best Super Hero He died and made me free!
Before He rose up from the grave**
(arms up in air)
Jesus beat the devil down!
(with fist hit other hand)
And one day He will put him in the ground, with FIRE, FIRE, FIRE!

Did you know that Jesus is the only way to know the love of Father?
(Listen to responses)

When you believed in Jesus, you became Father's son or daughter. As Father's child, you get to have fun as you obey Father and show Super Love to other people every day.

Get ready! We are going to make a Super Love T-shirt for you to wear and show love to others like Father and Jesus. Whenever you put on your T-shirt you must look for something SUPER NICE to do for someone else. But whether you are wearing it or not, let's agree to practice showing love and being kind to everyone!

If you agree, say, "I AGREE!"
(Listen to children's response)

MAKING A SUPER LOVE T-SHIRT:

Instructions:
1) Distribute pencils, eraser and paper to each child.
2) Tell the children to think of the design they want to draw on their T-shirt.
3) Children to draw draft of design with a pencil on paper. When child satisfied with their design draft, give child a T-Shirt to redraw their design in pencil on the T-Shirt.
4) After the design is on the T-Shirt in pencil, distribute the fabric markers for child to creatively color in their design.

IDEAS FOR CHILDREN TO PRACTICE LOVE:

Role Playing: Regularly, read to the children from a children's Bible and tell them stories of the things Jesus did. After reading about something Jesus did, discuss it to ensure the children understand, then encourage children to role play the things Jesus did.
(Provide props when possible)

Everyday Routine: As the child/ren go about their day, observe and let them know when you see them being kind and showing love to others.
(i.e. being patient, enjoying themselves and others (showing joy), helping others, etc.)

Be sure to document the good things observed on the last page of their "Student Progress Record."

Scriptures:
Isaiah 45:22; Isaiah 9:6; Isaiah 53:4-5; I John 4:7-12; Revelation 1:8; Colossians 2:13-15; Acts 1:9-10; Acts 2:21-24; Mark 1:11; Mark 1:30-34; Mark 6:12-13; Acts 4:12; John 14:12-14; Galatians 5:14; Galatians 6:10

P.A.C.E.
www.ABC-Jesus.com
© All Rights Reserved

FOLLOW UP ACTIVITY
COMMUNION JESUS IS OUR BREAD OF LIFE

Objectives to be Understood: Jesus is the Bread of life for our spirit, and we eat the bread and drink the juice to remember Him.

Materials: Bread, Crackers, Grape Juice, Cups, Napkins

Note to Parent/Teacher: The communion is only for the children that have received Jesus as their Lord either today or previously. For children that have not yet received Jesus, let them know they can have crackers and juice for their snack but must quietly eat while the children that were "Born Again" take communion to remember Jesus.

Parent/Teacher Script: Your body needs good food like bread to grow strong. Your spirit also needs good food to grow strong. Jesus said that Father sent him as our good bread of life. This means that like regular bread helps your body to grow strong, Jesus came and gave your spirit life, to be born again, and live forever by what he did for you. Jesus is our bread of life!
When we eat the bread, we need to remember what Jesus has done for us. What are some of the things you remember that Jesus did for us?

Answers could include:
Jesus died for our sins.
Jesus beat the devil for us.
We can be born again as heavenly Father's children!
Our spirit can live forever and not die.
Jesus took all sickness in his body so we don't have to be sick.

THE BREAD

Parent/Teacher Script: During the last supper that Jesus ate, before he went to the cross to die for our sins, Jesus asked that you do a certain thing to remember him. Jesus took some bread in his hands.
(Teacher takes bread in her hands)

He thanked his heavenly Father for the bread.
(Teacher gives thanks to our heavenly Father and breaks the bread, saying)

Then Jesus broke the bread into pieces and said, take, eat: this bread is my body which is given for you.
(Teacher gives each child a piece of bread to eat) Jesus said to do this to remember him.

Jesus is our bread of life.

THE GRAPE JUICE

Parent/Teacher Script:
And Jesus took the cup and when he had given thanks he gave it to them.
(Teacher gives thanks to our heavenly Father)
(Teacher gives each child a cup with a small amount of grape juice)

Jesus said Drink all of it, for this is my blood of the New Testament which is shed for many for the taking away of sins.

Do you understand why Jesus wanted you to eat bread as his body and drink grape juice as his blood? Jesus wanted us to remember him as our spiritual food like bread. When you drink the grape juice Jesus wanted you to remember that it was his blood that was poured out in exchange for your sins. So as you eat the bread and drink from the cup, you should remember Jesus, and love Him for what He did for you!

Scriptures:
I Corinthians 11:24-30; John 3:3-7; John 6:32-35, 6:51, 6:53, 6:55; Luke 22:19; Matthew 26:27-28; Romans 5:8-11

FOLLOW UP ACTIVITY
I HAVE ETERNAL LIFE TO LIVE FOREVER!

Objectives to be Understood: You do not have to die when you believe Jesus. You can pass from life on earth to life with Father and Jesus.

Materials: Worksheet entitled "These are some fun things I plan to do with Father and Jesus!"

Parent/Teacher Script:
Do you remember that Father made us a living soul, a spirit and a body?
(Listen to Responses)

Do you remember which part of you is the real you?
(Listen to Responses)

The real you is the part of you that you cannot see, your spirit and soul. Your spirit and soul live inside of your body. Jesus said it is the spirit that gives life. One day our bodies will die, but our spirit and soul will live forever with whoever you believed, either Jesus in heaven or the devil in hell. When you chose to believe Jesus, Father and Jesus gave you eternal life so you can know them and live forever with them in love. When Jesus was on earth he said, the Kingdom of God is like a little child.

What do you think He meant?
(Listen to Responses)

Jesus said, "Unless you turn to God from your sins and become as little children, you will never get into the Kingdom of heaven." God made little children to trust. In God's Kingdom we trust God as our Father who loves us. Since God's kingdom is like a little child, what do little children like to do?
(Listen to Responses)

Do you like to have fun?
(Listen to Responses)

Did you know that Father and Jesus like to have fun?
(Listen to Responses)

Jesus said He only did what He saw and heard His Father do. Jesus did some fun things. He went on boat rides. He walked on water. He would hike up mountains. Jesus was invited and went to a wedding with his friends. At many weddings, people dance, sing, laugh, eat good food, talk with friends and family, play games and have fun.

Children like to have fun. Jesus would not stop the children from coming to Him. Children love Jesus. Why do you think little children love Jesus? *(Listen to Responses)* Children know that Jesus loves them. Jesus prayed to Father for the children.

Parent/Teacher Script, (continued)**:**

Since you know that Father and Jesus like to have fun and they love you, what are some fun things that you would like to do with Father and Jesus?
(Listen to Responses)

Use your imagination and think of big things that only Father and Jesus could do with you. You might invite friends to have fun with you. Write or draw some fun things you plan to do with Father and Jesus since you can choose to live forever with them.

Scriptures:
I Thessalonians 5:23; Luke 18:16-17; 2 Corinthians 2:16; 2 Corinthians 5:8; I John 5:12-13; John 2:1-2; Matthew 18:3 (TLB); Matthew 8:1; Matthew 9:1; Matthew 14:25; John 8:29; John 17:3

These are some fun things I plan to do with Father and Jesus!

Written By: _____

Date: _____

FOLLOW UP ACTIVITY
WHAT DID GOD SAY? LESSON 3

Objectives to be Understood: For children to know:
1) God made you to be like Him;
2) God's Word is alive and true;
3) God's Word is like a sword;
4) God's Word has the power of life in it, and;
5) to say and pray what God has said.

Activity: Children will write in their books the Scriptures/Words God Said.

Important Note: This activity is included in each of our 6 lessons with a different scripture in each lesson for children to receive into their hearts.

Materials: Pencils; Markers; Stapler; Purchased notebooks OR Pre-made book template (see Preparation below)

Preparation: To MAKE A BOOK, Pre-make book templates for each child by folding two sheets of paper in half and stapling (two staples on the folded side so pages open like a book); OR purchase lined notebooks.
Write out and post (where children can easily see) the following scripture:

THE FATHER HAS LOVED US SO MUCH! THIS SHOWS HOW MUCH HE LOVED US: WE ARE CALLED CHILDREN OF GOD. AND WE REALLY ARE HIS CHILDREN. BUT THE PEOPLE IN THE WORLD DON'T UNDERSTAND THAT WE ARE GOD'S CHILDREN, BECAUSE THEY HAVE NOT KNOWN HIM.
I John 3:1 ERV

WHAT DID GOD SAY? LESSON 3 (continued):

REVIEW:
What happens when God speaks? *(Listen to responses)* Everything God says must happen!
Does God want you to believe the things He said? *(Listen to responses)*
God has given you His Words to believe Him and SAY WHAT HE HAS SAID. You were made to be like Father and speak Words that give life.
Different writers wrote what God told them to write in the Bible. The Words in the Bible are called scriptures. The Bible has different parts called books. The scripture that we will learn today can be found in the book of 1st John the third chapter and the 1st verse. I John 3:1
The Bible teaches us about God's love for us, and the things He had to do to send His Son Jesus to save us.

TO KNOW GOD'S WORD

First, you must LET YOUR EARS HEAR GOD'S WORD AND BELIEVE IT.
Second, LET YOUR MOUTH SAY THE WORDS THAT GOD HAS SAID.
Third, Tell your mind to THINK ABOUT WHAT GOD HAS SAID.
When you think about what God has said, HIS WORD GOES INSIDE YOUR HEART. And your heart will help you love like God.

If you would like God, your heavenly Father to help you to know Him and the Words He has said, you can pray and say these words after me, or you can pray to God in your own words. Ready. Let's pray!

PRAYER

Father,
(Pause for Children to Repeat)
I want to know You
(Pause)
Will you help me?
(Pause)
I want to hear and believe You
(Pause)
Will You teach me to say
(Pause)
what You have said every day?
(Pause)
Thank You Father!
(Pause)
Will you help me
(Pause)
to think about Your Word?
(Pause)
Thank You Father!
(Pause)
Will You let Your Word
(Pause)
change my heart
(Pause)
so I will love like You?
(Pause)
Thank You for hearing me
(Pause)
and answering my prayer!
(Pause)
I love You!
(Pause)
Amen.

WHAT DID GOD SAY? LESSON 3 (continued):

LEARNING SCRIPTURES FOR OUR BOOKS

Parent/Teacher Script:
Does anyone have something good to tell us that God did for you?
(Listen to the testimonies of the children)

We are going to add a new scripture to our What Did God Say books?
(Show children the Lesson 3 Scripture and let children know these are some Words God said.)

Our new scripture is: "The Father has loved us so much! This shows how much he loved us: We are called children of God. And we really are his children. But the people in the world don't understand that we are God's children, because they have not known him."

What do you think God means when He said, "The Father has loved us so much! This shows how much he loved us: We are called children of God. And we really are his children. But the people in the world don't understand that we are God's children, because they have not known him"?
(Listen to Responses)

Did you pray from your heart and ask Father to forgive your sins?
(Listen to Responses)

Did you tell God that you believed Jesus and that you wanted to be His child?
(Listen to Responses)

When you prayed and said words that you believed Jesus, Father forgave your sins and He made you His child. Father calls you His child.

Is everyone in the world God's child and know Him?
(Listen to Responses)

Does everyone in the world know that you are God's child?
(Listen to Responses)

No, many people in the world do not know God or understand how to love like Him, because they do not know Him. This is why He said, "The Father has loved us so much! This shows how much he loved us: We are called children of God. And we really are his children. But the people in the world don't understand that we are God's children, because they have not known him."

Parent/Teacher Script: (continued):

Let's boldly say His Words:
"**The Father has loved us so much!** *(children repeat)*
This shows how much He loved us: *(children repeat)*
We are called children of God. *(children repeat)*
And we really are His children. *(children repeat)*
But the people in the world, *(children repeat)*
don't understand, *(children repeat)*
that we are God's children, *(children repeat)*
because they have not known Him."
Let's say it again. ***(Repeat)***

Have you ever had someone to tell you they love you?
(Listen to responses)

Your Father in heaven loves you with a love that is not like the love on earth. His love is called agape love. Agape love is a heavenly amazing love.

Repeat after me!
My Father loves me (pause)
and He calls me His son or His daughter. I am a child of God.

Did you know that God's love is true? *(Listen to responses)* It is so true that the more you say what God has said, the power in God's words will go into your heart to live. And you will know the truth. And the truth is, God loves you!

Ask children to take out their books.
(CHILDREN WHO DID NOT BRING THEIR NOTE BOOKS, let them write their scripture on paper. Tell them to put it in their book when they get home.) (Provide notebooks for new children or make new book templates for this lesson.)

Write God's Words in your book.
Everyday read your book out loud and declare or say God's Words so your ears can Hear His Words!

Every day pay attention and watch Father do what He said because you believed Him, and you said what He said.

When you see Father do what He said, write or draw a picture in your book about the good things God did for you.
And come tell us about it.

(If children are using notebooks and want to take them home, remind them to bring their notebooks back so they can write more Words that God said in it.)

Let's Sing these Words God Said:
(Sing to the tune of "If you're happy and you know it")

**The Father has loved us so much!
The Father has loved us so much!
This shows how much He loved us.
And we really are His children.
But the people in the world don't understand.
(Declare) We're God's Children!**

(Repeat Several Times)

SONG: GOD LOVES ME!
(Sung to the tune of Barney Song)
(Do motions to Song)

YOU LOVE ME!
(Point upward, then to self)
I LOVE YOU!
(Point to self and upward)
YOU MAKE MY HEART GO PITTER-PAT!
(Point up, touch heart, Clap hands as you say pitter-pat)
YOU LOVED ME FIRST
(Point upward, then to self)
AND I LOVE YOU BACK!
(Kiss your hands and blow kisses up to Father)
YOU MAKE MY HEART GO PITTER-PAT!
(Point up, touch your heart, then clap hands as you say pitter-pat)
I LOVE YOU FATHER!
(Lift both hands up and SHOUT)

Scriptures:
I John 3:1; John 3:16; Romans 8:14-17

FOLLOW UP ACTIVITY
AWESOME HOLY SPIRIT!

Objectives to be Understood:
1) how Holy Spirit helps you;
2) you can pray and ask to receive the gift of Holy Spirit; and,
3) you can choose to speak in an unknown tongue.

Materials: None

Parent/Teacher Script:
Listen to how Awesome the Holy Spirit is!
Did you know that Jesus was born by the power of Holy Spirit?
God the Father sent an angel to a young woman named Mary and she said yes and let the Holy Spirit put the good seed of God in her for Jesus to be born on earth as a man and the Son of God.

Do you remember the name of the power of God that raised Jesus up from the dead?
(Listen to 'Responses)

It was the power of Holy Spirit that raised Jesus from the dead.
Did you know that God sent Holy Spirit to earth to live in you forever as One in Jesus?
(Listen to 'Responses)

When you ask Holy Spirit to live in you, you have the same power that raised Jesus from the dead in you!

Jesus prayed and Father answered His prayer and sent the power of His Holy Spirit to live in us forever as one in Jesus. Jesus and His Father are One. They are exactly alike. They think alike. Jesus does everything His Father says. And when you choose to obey Jesus, Holy Spirit will live in you as your Helper.

Do you know how Holy Spirit will Help you?
(Listen to 'Responses)

Holy Spirit will help you to know inside your heart what is true and what is not true.
Holy Spirit helps you to know that Father and Jesus are real and you can believe them.
Holy Spirit will help you to be a friend of Jesus.
Holy Spirit helps you to not be afraid.
Holy Spirit gives you the power to do the things you cannot do on your own.
Holy Spirit will help you to love God and others and do all the things that God planned for you to do on earth for Him.

Parent/Teacher Script: (continued):

Holy Spirit will help you to have a very good sound mind that thinks good thoughts.
Father knows that sometimes you do not know what to pray, but Holy Spirit will help you to pray in God's language of tongues the perfect will of God for you or someone else. Praying in tongues helps you to believe God more and more, every time you do it.

Raise your hand if you have already received the power of Holy Spirit to live with you and in you. *(Acknowledge those who have believed Jesus and received Holy Spirit)*

If you have not received Holy Spirit, and you believe Jesus, Jesus said that Father will give Holy Spirit to anyone who asks Him.

Do you want to receive the power of Holy Spirit as your Helper forever? *(Listen to Responses) (If anyone says Yes, then lead them in prayer to say they believe Jesus and ask Father to give them Holy Spirit. See Romans 10:9-10 or use the prayer for children to say I believe Jesus, in Story Book Lesson 3, JESUS)*

If you said you believe Jesus and received Holy Spirit, you can also pray directly to heavenly Father in His special language of tongues. If you choose we can pray together in tongues now. First let's talk to our heavenly Father to let Him know we received Holy Spirit and, we want to ask Him to help us speak directly to Him in Tongues. "Father, we received Holy Spirit. We ask that You give us Your spirit language of tongues. Amen" Let's thank Father. Thank you Father! Let's pray in God's heavenly language of Tongues now. Just open your mouth and say the sounds that come from your heart.

(Pray in Tongues!)

Praying in tongues is our secret weapon.

Scriptures:
Luke 1:30-38; Colossians 1:15; Galatians 3:19; John 14:7; John 14:16; John 17:20-23; John 14:15-16; John 14:20-21; I Corinthians 14:2; Jude 1:20; John 15:14; Romans 10:9; 2 Timothy 1:7; Romans 8:26-28; Luke 11:13;
I John 5:14-15

FOLLOW UP ACTIVITY
FATHER, SON, and HOLY SPIRIT!

Objectives to be Understood: For children to know Father, Son, and Holy Spirit are One God.

Materials: Container filled with water, cups, ice tray, pot, access to: a refrigerator/freezer and stove

Preparation: *(Have some ice made ahead to show children)*

Parent/Teacher Script:
How can Father, Son and Holy Spirit be One God? How can three be One?
(Listen to Responses)

Father is a BIG God! Father is bigger than our minds can think. We know some things that Father has told and shown us about Himself. Father is love. Father created all things. He is Almighty. He is Holy. Nothing or no one is greater, smarter or better than Him. We know that Father created the universe through His powerful Word. Do you remember who Father calls The Word?
(Listen to Responses)

Father's Son, Jesus, is His Word. Jesus is The Word of God. Father created the universe through Jesus. Jesus is the Word that Father sends out from Himself. Jesus and Father are One Spirit. Father is a powerful Spirit. Do you remember what the name of Father's power is called?
(Listen to Responses)

Holy Spirit is Father's power. Holy Spirit is the Power that Father sends out from Himself. Holy Spirit is also One with God.

Father, Jesus His Son, and Holy Spirit are three parts of One God. They each do different things. Have you ever seen something that has three parts but is one thing?
(Listen to Responses)

Let's do an experiment with water to see how God made water to do three different things as one.
(Show children the water as you pour it into a cup.)

<u>Ask children:</u> What is this called?
(Listen to Responses)

We call this WATER.
(Pour a little water into cups for children to drink.)

86

Parent/Teacher Script: (continued):

When the water is a liquid, we can pour it into cups and drink it. The water helps our bodies to be healthy. Let's see how water is three in one.
(Show children as you pour water into an ice tray and put it into the freezer of a refrigerator.)
(Show children the water that has hardened into ice after it freezes.)

<u>Tell the children</u>: The ice is still water but it is frozen water that we call ICE.
(Put some ice in the children's cups for them to hold and eat if they choose.)

When the water is ice, the water does something different. It makes things cold for us.
What happens to the ice when it melts?
(Listen to Responses)

It becomes water again.
So far we have seen the water as two things. First we saw the water as a liquid that we could drink, and second we saw the water as ice.
Let's see the third thing the water can be.
(Show the children as you pour water into a pot to boil on the stove.)

<u>Tell children</u>: Watch to see what happens to the water when it begins to boil.
(When the water begins to boil and steam forms)

<u>Tell children</u>: We call the vapor coming up from the water STEAM. It is still water but it is now in the form of steam.
Now you can see how one thing can have three forms. One, as a liquid, it is water. Two, when it's frozen, it is ice. Third, when we heat the water to boiling, it becomes steam.
God made some things to be three in one.
God is also three in one.
He is Father, Son and Holy Spirit!

Scriptures:
Deuteronomy 6:4; I John 5:7; John 17:21-22; John 4:24; John 14:10; Hebrews 1:2-3; Acts 1:8

FORGIVE
(Read Book 4)

PARENT LETTER 4

Dear Parents,
We are using the Foundation Curriculum in partnership with you. Please review (a minimum of three to six times) with your child the lesson entitled "FORGIVE." The story emphasizes how heavenly Father's "Born Again" children can choose to *do things like* their heavenly Father and Jesus, by forgiving others!

We discussed that to love others, does not mean you have to let someone mistreat you and hurt you because your heavenly Father loves you and does not want *anyone* to harm or mistreat you; but they can pray and ask for wisdom *(James 1:5)* and Holy Spirit in them will give them wisdom, and they will know what to say and do.
(I Peter 3:12)

Please help your child to understand this scripture from Romans 12:18-21 "If possible live in peace with everyone. Do that as much as you can. My friends don't try to get even. Leave room for God to show His anger. It is written, "I am the One who judges people. I will pay them back," says the Lord. "Do just the opposite." Scripture says, "If your enemies are hungry, give them food to eat. If they are thirsty, give them something to drink. By doing these things, you will pile up burning coals on their heads. Don't let evil overcome you. Overcome evil by doing good."

This teaching to forgive, which is God's way, opposes the world's philosophy of an eye for an eye and a tooth for a tooth. (Matthew 5:38-48) Your child heard that Jesus said that if we do not forgive others, that our Father will not forgive us. (Matthew 6:14-15) We know that sometimes it is hard to forgive, but when we pray in the name of Jesus and ask Father to help us to forgive, Jesus will change our heart that Father may receive the glory. (John 14:13) Holy Spirit helps us. *(John 14:16)*

We practiced love by praying for those who have hurt us and sinned against us.
(Matthew 5:44-45)

Please let your child/ren know that to do things heavenly Father's way, in love and forgiveness, it does not make them weak, but strong in the love of Jesus for they are reflecting heavenly Father's perfect image of love! *(I John 4:7-12; Matthew 5:46-48)* God bless you as you teach your child/ren true wisdom *(Psalm 111:10)* to obey God, and overcome evil with good!

Sincerely yours in Christ Jesus,

Your Child's Teacher
Contact information: _____

P.A.C.E.
www.ABC-Jesus.com
© All Rights Reserved

FOLLOW UP ACTIVITIES

FOLLOW UP ACTIVITY
FATHER HAS FORGIVEN ME SONG

Objectives to be Understood: Father has forgiven all of our sins because of Jesus.

Materials: None

Parent/Teacher Script: God is love! He is Holy and He does things right! God does not sin. God does not want His children to sin. God, our heavenly Father made a law that sin was a crime and, everyone who sinned must die. Do you know what that means?
(Listen to Response)

It means that you, me and everyone would have to die because of the bad things we have done. Heavenly Father loved us so much that He sent Jesus to earth to die in our place. Instead of you and me getting what we deserved for disobeying God and sinning, Jesus came and died for ALL of our sins.

What do you think God did when Jesus let people beat and kill Him *instead* of you and me?
(Listen to Responses)

God our Father forgave us because of what Jesus did! Jesus told us to forgive others also or our Father in heaven will not forgive us.

Let's sing the "Father has forgiven me" song.
(Sing to the tune of *I Am Special*; Or make up your own tune!)
(*Fold your hands as in prayer*)

Thank you Jesus! Thank you Jesus!
(*Point upwards*)
Father forgave me!
Father forgave me!
(*Point to yourself*)
You took my sins upon you!
You took my sins upon you!
(*Throw your hands up in joy*)
Now I'm free! Now I'm free!

Scriptures:
Romans 6:23; Romans 3:23; Romans 5:8-10; Hebrews 10:12-18; Romans 6:22

FOLLOW UP ACTIVITY
THE FORGIVE EXERCISE!

Objectives to be Understood: Heavenly Father and Jesus commanded us to forgive everyone.

Instructions:
1) Parent/Teacher asks for one child to tell how s/he would handle a situation that will be read. (The child waits as the group sings The Forgive Song)
    a. The group sings The Forgive Song (Part 1) to the child.
       (Parent/Teacher to help all children learn the words to the Forgive Song)
2) After Part 1 of the song is sung, the parent/teacher reads a situation aloud.
3) Child tells how s/he would handle the situation.
   (Encourage the group to give their responses also.)
4) If the child chooses TO FORGIVE:
    a. The parent/teacher leads the class as they all clap for the child's good choice.
    b. The parent/teacher leads the class (to learn) to sing The Forgive Song (Part 2) inserting the child's name into the song.
5) If the child chooses NOT to FORGIVE:
6) The teacher should gently remind the child of how Jesus told us to forgive others when they sin against us and to pray for the people who despitefully use us; and we can ask heavenly Father to help us to forgive.
7) Repeat instructions, using a different child and a different situation card.

The Forgive Song (Part 1)
(To the tune of: This is my story, this is my song; praising my Savior all the day long; OR make up your own tune!)

**This is what happened. What will you do?
Will you forgive them, like Jesus told you?
This is what happened. What will you do?
Will you forgive them, like Jesus told you?**

The Forgive Song (Part 2)
(To the tune of: This is my story, this is my song; praising my Savior all the day long; OR make up your own tune!)

**____ forgave them, s/he showed love today.
____ forgave them, s/he did it God's way.
____ forgave them, s/he showed love today.
____ forgave them, s/he did it God's way.**

IMPORTANT NOTE TO PARENT/TEACHER REGARDING SITUATION CARDS

Some *Guidance* has been given in each situation to assist in the facilitation of a discussion with the child and the group about the many varying aspects of each situation. It is always best however to follow the guidance of Holy Spirit.

Scriptures:
Matthew 6:14-15; Matthew 5:44; Mark 14:65

Situation 1

(Sing with group the Forgive Song 1)
(To the tune of: This is my story, this is my song; praising my Savior all the day long;
OR make up your own tune!)

This is what happened. What will you do?
Will you forgive them, like Jesus told you?

<u>Parent/Teacher reads:</u> A person that you wanted to be friends with said some bad things about you. Your feelings are hurt. What is the first thing that you would do?
(Parent/Teacher to listen carefully to answer)

Parent/Teacher Guidance:
<u>Ask:</u> Would you say anything to the person? (wait for volunteer to respond)
<u>Ask:</u> Why? (or) Why not? (listen to response)
<u>Ask:</u> Would you still want to be friends with the person? (listen to volunteer's response)
<u>Ask:</u> Why? (or) Why not?
<u>Say:</u> You have a choice to make here. You can treat this person mean and keep feeling bad about what they said about you. Or, you can do what Jesus did, before he went to the cross to give his life in exchange for our sins. The people mocked Jesus and made fun of Him. They beat Him with a whip and ripped the flesh off His bones. They spit on Him but he did not say anything. He was not offended because he knew that they did not know any better. Jesus knew they did not know the love of his Father, and therefore said in prayer, Father forgive them; for they know not what they do. Remember God's way is love.
Ask: What did Jesus say to do? (listen to child's response)
Ask: Will you forgive the person who hurt your feelings and pray for them like Jesus did? (listen to child's response)

(If volunteer chose to forgive, sing the Forgive Song 2, inserting the volunteer's name in the blank.)
(To the tune of: This is my story, this is my song; praising my Savior all the day long.)

____ forgave them, s/he showed love today.
____ forgave them, s/he did it God's way.
____ forgave them, s/he showed love today.
____ forgave them, s/he did it God's way.

(If child chooses not to forgive, gently remind the child of what Jesus said.)

Jesus told us to forgive others when they sin against you and to pray for them who despitefully use you.
Thank you_____ (volunteer's name) for volunteering.

Situation 2
(Sing with group the Forgive Song 1)
(To the tune of: This is my story, this is my song; praising my Savior all the day long; OR make up your own tune!)

**This is what happened. What will you do?
Will you forgive them, like Jesus told you?**

<u>Parent/Teacher reads:</u> You were walking home and a mean girl spit on you and said you think you are better than me. What is the first thing that you would do?
(Parent/Teacher to listen carefully to answer)

Parent/Teacher Guidance:
<u>Ask:</u> Why? (listen to response)
<u>Say:</u> I know you would probably be angry that she spit on you, or think that you had to do something to get even. But remember who you are. You are a child of heavenly Father, the Most-High God. And God loves her too; and you now have an opportunity to show her the love of God. *(Parent/Teacher to listen to response)*
<u>Ask:</u> How could you respond to the girl in love like Jesus taught? (wait for volunteer and/or group to respond)
<u>Say:</u> You could pray quickly inside your heart and ask Holy Spirit to guide you in what you say and do next. For it is obvious that the girl does not know about God's way of doing things. Otherwise she would not have spit on you.
<u>Ask:</u> Can you think of anything you could say to her in love, God's way? (listen to child's response and ask group)
<u>Ask:</u> What did Jesus say to do? (listen to volunteer's response)
<u>Say:</u> More than one person spit on Jesus, and they hit him with the palms of their hands when he was going to the cross to give his life so that we all could know our heavenly Father, and he forgave them.
<u>Ask:</u> Will you forgive the person who spit on you and pray for her like Jesus did? (listen to volunteer and group's response)

(If volunteer chose to forgive, sing the Forgive Song 2, inserting the volunteer's name in the blank.)
(To the tune of: This is my story, this is my song; praising my Savior all the day long.)

____ forgave them, s/he showed love today.
____ forgave them, s/he did it God's way.♪
____ forgave them, s/he showed love today.
____ forgave them, s/he did it God's way.

(If child chooses not to forgive, gently remind the child of what Jesus said.)

Jesus told us to forgive others when they sin against you and to pray for them who despitefully use you.
Thank you_____ (volunteer's name) for volunteering.

P.A.C.E.
www.ABC-Jesus.com
© All Rights Reserved

Situation 3

(Sing with group the Forgive Song 1)
*(To the tune of: This is my story, this is my song; praising my Savior all the day long;
OR make up your own tune!)*

**This is what happened. What will you do?
Will you forgive them, like Jesus told you?**

<u>Parent/Teacher reads:</u> A boy that you thought was a friend stuck out his foot and tripped you. You fell and hurt your knee. It was bleeding. What would you say or do?
(Parent/Teacher to listen carefully to answer)

Parent/Teacher Guidance:
<u>Ask:</u> Why? (listen to response)
<u>Ask:</u> Would you still want to be friends with him? (listen to response)
<u>Ask:</u> Why? or Why not? (listen to response)
<u>Ask:</u> What did Jesus say to do? (listen to response)
<u>Ask:</u> Would you forgive the person who hurt you and pray for him like Jesus said? (listen to response)
<u>Say:</u> Sometimes forgiving someone is not the first thing we think of when someone hurts us. The way most people would try to handle this situation is to be mean right back or to get revenge. But Jesus said that the blood that he shed (on the cross) was to give you a new covenant promise from heavenly Father; that by the blood of Jesus, your heavenly Father would forgive your sins and remember them no more. (Matthew 26:28; Hebrew 8:10-13) Your heavenly Father doesn't want any one to hurt you and has said, "Vengeance *is* mine!" Your heavenly Father will repay them for the evil done to you. (Romans 12:19) God said to overcome evil with good. (Romans 12:20-21)
<u>Ask:</u> To handle this situation the way God said, can you (or anyone) think of what you could say to the boy? (listen to responses)
<u>Say:</u> You could pray quickly and silently and ask for just the right words. Then speak and trust Jesus. When you trust God, what you say and what you do will be right. Remember you are a child of God and your heavenly Father wants you to show others how to live in love.
<u>Ask:</u> Do you think you can do that? (listen to response) (If children say YES, tell them good job for that is what heavenly Father and Jesus commanded.)   (If children say NO, let them know that sometimes we have to pray and trust Holy Spirit to help us when we know we cannot do it ourselves; because Jesus and heavenly Father had given you the power of Holy Spirit to overcome all tough situations. With the help of Holy Spirit, you can do it!) (Acts 1:8)

(If volunteer chose to forgive, sing the Forgive Song 2, inserting the volunteer's name in the blank.)
(To the tune of: This is my story, this is my song; praising my Savior all the day long.)

   **____ forgave them, s/he showed love today.
   ____ forgave them, s/he did it God's way.
   ____ forgave them, s/he showed love today.
   ____ forgave them s/he did it God's way.**

(If child chooses not to forgive, gently remind the child of what Jesus said.)

Jesus told us to forgive others when they sin against you and to pray for them who despitefully use you.
Thank you_____ (volunteer's name) for volunteering.

P.A.C.E.
www.ABC-Jesus.com
© All Rights Reserved

Situation Card 4

(Sing with group the Forgive Song 1)
*(To the tune of: This is my story, this is my song; praising my Savior all the day long;
OR make up your own tune!)*

**This is what happened. What will you do?
Will you forgive them, like Jesus told you?**

<u>Parent/Teacher reads</u>: A tall boy whispered to you that he was going to beat you up. What is the first thing that you would say or do? *(Parent/Teacher to listen carefully and respond)*

Parent/Teacher Guidance:
<u>Ask</u>: (the group) Has anything like this ever happened to you? (listen to answers)
<u>Ask</u>: (dependent on response) What did you do? (listen to responses)
<u>Ask</u>: (volunteer and group) Were you or would you be afraid? (listen to responses)
<u>Ask</u>: Does anyone know what the Word of God says about fear, or being afraid of any thing? (listen to responses)
<u>Say</u>: The Word of God says that God has not given us a spirit of fear, but of power of love and of a sound mind. (II Timothy 1:7)
<u>Ask</u>: What do you think that means? (listen to responses)
<u>Say</u>: God does not lie. (Titus 1:2) So when His Word says that He has not given us a spirit of fear, you say what God says about you. So tell yourself, no matter what the situation is, that you are NOT afraid. Can you do that? (listen to responses)
<u>Say</u>: Let's say it together. Say, I am not afraid! (Say with children, I am not afraid!) That's right! God has not given you a spirit of fear, but of power, love and a sound mind. (repeat the verse together) God has not given me the spirit of fear, but of power, love and a sound mind. (2 Tim. 1:7)
<u>Say</u>: The next thing God's Word said in that scripture was that God has given us a spirit of power, love and a sound mind. The power we have from God is Holy Spirit who helps us to do all things like Jesus. (Acts 1:8) So when we do things like Jesus, how do we do things? (listen to responses)
<u>Say</u>: We do things God's way, in love! (I John 4:16) For there is no fear in love, because when you show love, fear is tossed out the door. (I John 4:18) Also God said we have a sound mind. A sound mind is a mind at peace because you know you are doing things like Jesus.
<u>Say</u>: So let's get back to the situation. This bully has said that he was going to beat you up. What did Jesus say to do? (listen to child's response) <u>Say</u>:
Jesus told us to pray for those who despitefully use you—those who do you wrong. You can show this person love by praying for him and obeying God.
<u>Say</u>: (to volunteer) You heard what Jesus said. Do you believe that God can change this person's heart? (listen to response)
<u>Say</u>: God can change anyone's heart but someone must ask. Will you do it? Will you forgive him for being mean and pray that God changes his heart? (listen to child's and group's response, and commend children for choosing God's way, or remind of what Jesus said.)

(If volunteer chose to forgive, sing the Forgive Song 2, inserting the volunteer's name in the blank.)
(To the tune of: This is my story, this is my song; praising my Savior all the day long)

**____ forgave them, s/he showed love today.
____ forgave them, s/he did it God's way.
____ forgave them, s/he showed love today.
____ forgave them, s/he did it God's way.**

(If child chooses not to forgive, gently remind the child of what Jesus said.)

Jesus told us to forgive others when they sin against you and to pray for them who despitefully use you. Thank you_____ (volunteer's name) for volunteering.

P.A.C.E.
www.ABC-Jesus.com
© All Rights Reserved

Situation Card 5
(Sing with group the Forgive Song 1)
(To the tune of: This is my story, this is my song; praising my Savior all the day long)

This is what happened. What will you do?
Will you forgive them, like Jesus told you?

<u>Parent/Teacher reads:</u> As you walked towards a group of people talking, you smiled and said hello. One person cursed and called you this awful name. They all laughed. What would you say or do? *(Parent/Teacher to listen carefully to response)*

Parent/Teacher Guidance:
<u>Ask:</u> (the group) Has this or something like this ever happened to any of you? (listen to responses) (if so, ask) What did you do?
<u>Say:</u> It is not easy to have someone curse or laugh at you. Is it? (listen to responses) In this case your feelings might be hurt because of what the person said and how the group acted.
<u>Ask:</u> If I call you a rat, does that make you a rat? (listen to responses)
<u>Say:</u> No, you are still (call each child by name). The Word of God said that you are wondrously made. God chose to make you look like you look. You are His beloved. Created in His image! God loves you, and has blessed you because of what Jesus did for you on the cross. People who say cursing words and mock others do not yet know your heavenly Father's heart of love. Remember, Jesus showed us how to love others, even when others act ignorant; for when Jesus was going to the cross people mocked Jesus, but he blessed them all by dying for the sins of everyone, even the people who don't know about his love yet. Jesus blessed those who cursed and hated him and prayed for them that despitefully used him, and persecuted him. Therefore, although your feelings may be hurt, we have to put our feelings aside and remember what Jesus did and commanded us to do.
<u>Ask:</u> (the volunteer and group) You have a choice to make. What are some things that you could say or do that would show God's love? (listen to responses and guide the discussion, commending and reminding the children of how heavenly Father and Jesus commanded us to respond)

(If volunteer chose to forgive, sing the Forgive Song 2, inserting the volunteer's name in the blank.)
(To the tune of: This is my story, this is my song; praising my Savior all the day long.)

____ forgave them, s/he showed love today.
____ forgave them, s/he did it God's way.
____ forgave them, s/he showed love today.
____forgave them, s/he did it God's way.

(If child chooses not to forgive, gently remind the child of what Jesus said.)

Jesus told us to forgive others when they sin against you and to pray for them who despitefully use you.
Thank you_____ (volunteer's name) for volunteering.

FOLLOW UP ACTIVITY
YOU ARE A KING AND AMBASSADOR

Objectives to be Understood: when you believed Jesus, you become one of Father's children, a king in Christ Jesus, and an ambassador on earth to show and tell others about Father's love for them.

Activity: Children will make crowns to remind them that as children of God, He has made them kings and ambassadors in their spirit.

Materials: crown pattern; tag board; markers; crayons; scissors; stapler; tape, yarn or ribbon, hole puncher, glue sticks; aluminum foil; jewel-like stickers; other glittery materials to put on a crown.

Parent/Teacher Script: Father is a Spirit. Holy Spirit is a Spirit. When Jesus rose from the dead, Father gave Jesus a new Spirit body. Your spirit lives inside of your body. When you believed Jesus, Father made you a totally new person in your spirit, and gave you Holy Spirit to live in you and be with you. Father is King of the universe and the highest King of all things. When you believed Jesus, Father made you His child and a king on the earth in your spirit. Jesus is the King over all of God's kings on the earth. Jesus has given you a mission and a job to do on earth for Father. Your work for God is to be His king and ambassador. Do you know what an ambassador does?

An ambassador is a person that is sent somewhere by their King to say and do what their King told them. Your mission and job as king and ambassador is to believe Jesus and show Father's love to all people. Raise your hand if you accept the mission to be God's king and ambassador on earth.

Let's say it together:

"YES! I AM A KING AND AMBASSADOR FOR JESUS!"
(Repeat several times with power!)

In the spirit, God has given His sons and daughters crowns. We don't know what your crown looks like but we know it is beautiful. We will make crowns to remind us that God has made His children that believe Jesus, kings and ambassadors in our brand new spirit. And we have a job to do for God on earth!

P.A.C.E.
www.ABC-Jesus.com
© All Rights Reserved

INSTRUCTIONS TO MAKE A CROWN:

1. Cut out (from sturdy paper, i.e. tag board) a crown for each child. *(See crown pattern or make your own crown pattern)*
2. Provide materials for children to decorate their crowns.
3. As children make their crowns, tell them:

    They have the job of showing others Father's Kingdom of love.
    This is fun and makes Father and Jesus happy.
    You get to tell others that Father and Jesus loves them.
    You can tell them what Jesus did for all of us.
    You can pray for others.
    When people say or do mean things you can forgive them like Jesus.
    Holy Spirit is your helper and together Holy Spirit and you have a great job to do!

4. Ask children: Since you are an ambassador for Jesus, what are some things that you can do to show love to others? *(Listen to responses)*

Scriptures:
2 Corinthians 5:18-21; I Timothy 6:15; Isaiah 33:22; Jeremiah 10:10; John 4:24;
Revelation 1:5-6

CROWN PATTERN

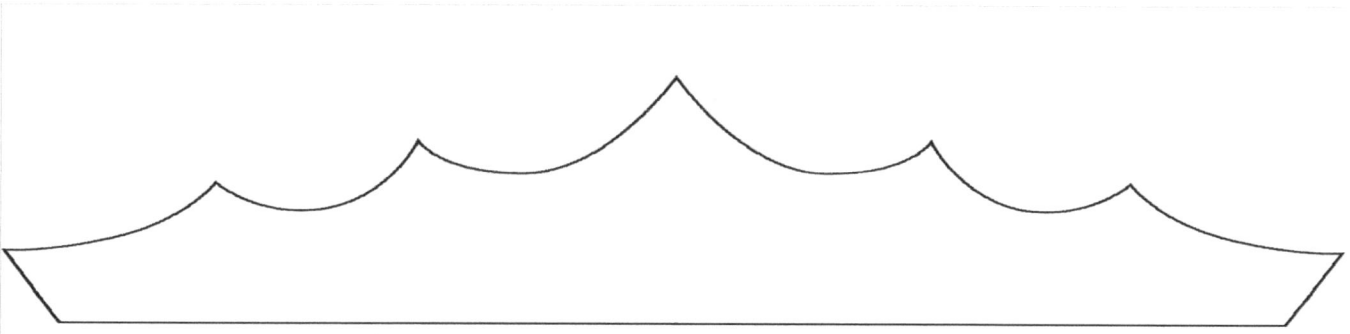

1) Cut out crown.
2) Child to decorate crown.
3) To attach sides of crown to rest on child's head, either:
    a. Punch a hole in each side of crown, tie yarn or ribbon through holes, and tie yarn or ribbon ends at back of child's head. Or,
    b. tape or staple paper strips to sides of crown, measure tag board strips to size of child's head, and tape the strips together so that crown rests on child's head.

Crown Pattern used from internet site Pattern of child crown – Bing Images.htm

FOLLOW UP ACTIVITY
FRUIT OF THE SPIRIT

Objectives to be Understood: You can set your mind on the things of the Spirit and be led by the Spirit, and bring forth the Fruit of the Spirit of Jesus.

Materials: Basket or container; the names of the fruit of the Spirit written on slips of paper; unlined paper; crayons; markers; pencils; See Variation.

Parent/Teacher Script:
The Word of God says, "…those who identify with the Spirit set their minds on the things of the Spirit." Romans 8:5 What do you think that means?
(Listen to Responses)

It means when you truly know that you are a child of God (God is a Spirit) you should set your mind to think about the things of the Spirit of God so Holy Spirit can lead you and help you. Everyone who is led by the Holy Spirit is God's son. To be led by the Holy Spirit is to set your mind to remember that you are God's son or daughter—and know Holy Spirit will help you to choose to do the right thing to bear much fruit. Did you know there is fruit inside Holy Spirit?
(Listen to Responses)

It is not the fruit that grows on trees. The fruit in Holy Spirit is called the Fruit of the Spirit. What do you think the Fruit of the Spirit is?
(Listen to Responses)

The fruit is things the Holy Spirit will give you to help you to obey Jesus.

Jesus wants you to let Holy Spirit lead you and help you make good choices. Jesus does NOT want you to let your feelings be your leader. Sometimes what you feel will NOT be what Jesus said. Jesus told us two commands from the Words Father spoke. Jesus told us to LOVE Father first with all of our heart, with all our soul, and with all of our strength. And also to LOVE other people just like you love yourself. These are the two big things that Jesus has commanded us to do. Sometimes loving other people on the earth is hard because everyone is not nice. Sometimes you might feel like doing something or saying something that is NOT nice or the right way God told His children to love. But Holy Spirit makes it easy and helps you. He gives you the Fruit of the Spirit, which is what you need to truly love other people and show them God's love.

Remember, when you choose to THINK about the things of the Spirit, and you choose to obey the Words Jesus said, you are being led by the Spirit. Then Holy Spirit who is in you and with you will help you to bear much fruit.

Activity Directions:
1) Give each child paper. Set out markers, crayons and pencils.
2) Ask each child to pull the name of a "Fruit of the Spirit" from the basket.
3) Read the "Description of Fruit of the Spirit" that the child pulls.
4) Tell child to draw a picture of them-self showing the fruit. For example, "kindness' could be a drawing of you helping someone. "Self-Control" could be a drawing of you NOT hitting someone, etc.
5) Tell children the fruit they pulled is their special fruit to practice for the week.
6) Their assignment is for each child to look for ways to let other people see their fruit. After the week is over, children are to return and talk about what happened.
7) To help children become aware of each of the nine fruits of the spirit, continue this activity over nine weeks letting children pull a different fruit from the basket weekly to practice. (If the same fruit is chosen from basket by a child let them pick again until they select a different fruit.) Ask "The Questions" each week. ("The Questions" are located at the end of this activity)
8) Document on the last two pages of the "Student Progress Record" the Fruit of the Spirit that you observed the child doing, in addition to the information the child shares.

Variation: Make a "Fruit of the Spirit" tree. Make enough removable pictures of fruit to go on the tree for each child to have at least one. Write the name of a Fruit of the Spirit on each fruit. *(use two-sided tape to tape picture of fruit onto tree)* Instead of using the basket to pick a fruit, let children take a fruit from the tree. Continue to follow Activity Directions.

DESCRIPTION OF FRUIT OF THE SPIRIT
This is how Holy Spirit helps you to bear much fruit.

LOVE: Whenever you need help to love someone, Holy Spirit will help you to bear the fruit of **Love**. If you don't want to love the person, think about how much Jesus and Father love them. Think about how the person may not know about God's love. Pray and talk to Father. Ask Him to help you. What do you believe will happen when you ask for help? *(Listen to Responses)* Holy Spirit will help you and put the fruit of the love of God in your heart! Then you can choose to love instead of following how you feel.

JOY: Holy Spirit has the fruit of **Joy** in Him! Joy is being happy inside no matter what is happening around you because of Jesus. When you keep the joy of the Lord Jesus in your heart it makes you strong. When you feel sad and need help to keep your joy, remember Holy Spirit is with you, so ask Father to help you keep His joy in your heart. What do you believe will happen when you ask for help? *(Listen to Responses)* Holy Spirit will help you and put the fruit of the joy of the Lord Jesus in your heart!

PEACE: Holy Spirit has the fruit of **Peace** in Him. When people around you are upset or angry, you don't have to be upset or angry because you have the PEACE of Jesus in you! When you need help to keep your peace, who is your helper with you? *(Listen to Responses)* Holy Spirit is your helper. So ask Father to help you keep His peace in your heart. What do you believe will

happen when you ask for help? *(Listen to Responses)* Holy Spirit will help you and put the fruit of the peace of God in your heart! Remember to thank God.

PATIENCE: Father knew that sometimes you will have to wait for some things. So the fruit of **Patience** is in the Spirit for you. If you feel like you cannot wait for something to happen, just remember Jesus and your helper, Holy Spirit. Ask Father to help you to be patient and wait until it's your turn. What do you believe will happen when you ask for help? *(Listen to Responses)* Holy Spirit will help you to be patient!

KINDNESS: The fruit of **Kindness** is in Holy Spirit. Have you ever seen someone who was being mean? *(Listen to Responses)* Jesus wants you to show love and be kind. If you need help to be kind and choose to do the right thing, think about the things of the Spirit. Ask Father to help you to be kind, and Holy Spirit will put the fruit of kindness in your heart.

GOODNESS: The fruit of **Goodness** is in Holy Spirit. Father is good and He does everything right. When Jesus came to earth, He showed us how to do good things God's way. As a child of Father, you should look for ways to show the goodness of God to others every day. So when you see someone that needs something good that you can do for them, and you need help *to want* to do it, pray and ask Father. And what will Father do? *(Listen to Responses)* Holy Spirit will help the fruit of God's goodness to come in your heart!

FAITHFULNESS: The fruit of **Faithfulness** is also in Holy Spirit. Even though Jesus could choose if He would obey Father or not, Jesus was faithful and obeyed and did everything that Father told Him to do. Father could trust Jesus. Jesus wants you to obey Him and show others Father's love. But if you need help to be faithful, what should you do? *(Listen to Responses)* Pray and ask Father. And what will happen when you pray? *(Listen to Responses)* Holy Spirit will help the fruit of faithfulness to come into your heart.

HUMILITY: God has the fruit of **Humility**. Humility means that you treat others with respect and are not rude. You are polite, humble, and thank others for the good they do. When someone yells, fights or is mean hearted, you can choose not to yell, fight or be mean in your heart. To be humble means that you have inner strength to be quiet when others are rude and being mean. Jesus told you to pray for those who are rude and mean and show His love to them. Holy Spirit has the strength of the humility of Jesus. But if you want to hurt the person instead of showing humility, what should you do instead? *(Listen to Responses)* Pray and ask Father to help, and Holy Spirit will help the fruit of humility to come in your heart.

SELF-CONTROL: God has the fruit of **Self-Control** for you. Self-control means that you have the strength and power to control yourself and be the leader of how you feel. If someone calls you a bad name, you can control yourself and NOT get angry because when people say or do bad things it means they do NOT know Father's love or they are not thinking about it. Jesus does not want you to be angry at anyone and let the sun go down that day. If you feel anger at them, do not do any bad thing. What could you do instead? *(Listen to Responses)* Pray and ask Father! And who will help you? *(Listen to Responses)* Holy Spirit will help the fruit of Self-Control to come into you.

THE QUESTIONS:
1) <u>What must you do to be "Led by the Spirit?"</u> *(Listen to Responses)*
   a. To be led by the Spirit, you must set your mind to THINK about Spirit things.

2) <u>How do you set your mind to think about Spirit things?</u> *(Listen to Responses)*
   a. All day, whenever you have choices to make and things to say--THINK--and remember you are a child of God. Ask yourself, what would Jesus want me to do? What would Jesus want me to say? Pray to Father! Think about Holy Spirit in you and with you to help you. Thinking about Father, Jesus, and Holy Spirit is how you keep your mind on the things of the Spirit and bear much fruit when you choose to obey God!

Fruit of the Spirit Song!

I have <u>LOVE</u> inside of me.
Do-Daw! Do-Daw!
It's growing BIG just like a tree. Because I show <u>LOVE</u> today!
OH, I'LL SHOW <u>LOVE</u> TODAY!
I'LL SHOW <u>LOVE</u> TODAY!
When I show <u>LOVE</u> it grows in me.
SO I'LL SHOW <u>LOVE</u> TODAY!

<u>ASK</u>: What is another fruit that Father put inside of your "Born Again" Spirit?
(Listen to Responses)

Repeat Song: Each time replacing the word **LOVE** for a different Fruit of the Spirit:
- **JOY;**
- **PEACE;**
- **PATIENCE;**
- **GENTLENESS;**
- **GOODNESS;**
- **FAITH;**
- **MEEKNESS;**
- **SELF-CONTROL**

Scriptures:
Romans 8:4-6; Romans 8:14-16; John 15:5-7; Galatians 5:16-23; Jude 1:20; John 3:7; Matthew 5:44; Romans 12:17-21; John 14:26; John 15:5-8; I Thessalonians 5:17; Ephesians 4:26

P.A.C.E.
www.ABC-Jesus.com
© All Rights Reserved

FOLLOW UP ACTIVITY
WHAT DID GOD SAY? LESSON 4

Objectives to be Understood: For children to know:
1) God made you to be like Him;
2) God's Word is alive and true;
3) God's Word is like a sword;
4) God's Word has the power of life in it, and;
5) to say what God has said.

ACTIVITY: Children will write in their books the Scriptures/Words God Said.

IMPORTANT NOTE: This activity is included in each of our 6 lessons with a different scripture in each lesson for children to receive into their hearts.

MATERIALS: Pencils; Markers; Stapler; Pre-made book template or purchased notebooks (see Preparation below)

Preparation: To MAKE A BOOK
Pre-make book templates for each child by folding two sheets of paper in half and stapling (two staples on the folded side so pages open like a book); OR purchase lined notebooks.

Write out and post (where children can easily see) the following scripture:

DON'T LET EVIL DEFEAT YOU, BUT DEFEAT EVIL BY DOING GOOD.
Romans 12:21

P.A.C.E.
www.ABC-Jesus.com
© All Rights Reserved

REVIEW:

1) Are God's Words alive or dead?   (Listen to Responses)
   a. Answer: God's Words are ALIVE and TRUE. God made everything to be good and come alive by His Word. Everything God says must happen! God can not lie.
2) Why is it very important that you learn the things that God has said in the Bible? (Listen to responses)
   a. Answer: Father made you to be like Him, in His image. The Holy Bible has God's Words in it so you can learn what He said and to be like Him.
3) Different writers wrote what God told them to write in the Bible. What are the Words in the Bible called? Answer: The Words in the Bible are called scriptures.
4) What are the different parts of the Bible called? Answer: Books. The scripture that we will learn today can be found in the book of Romans the twelfth chapter and the 21rd verse. Romans 12:21
   a. The Bible has stories about God, and Words God said that are written down for you to know God and His love for you.

TO KNOW GOD'S WORD

First, you must LET YOUR EARS HEAR GOD'S WORD AND BELIEVE IT.
Second, LET YOUR MOUTH SAY THE WORDS THAT GOD HAS SAID.
Third, Tell your mind to THINK ABOUT WHAT GOD HAS SAID.
When you think about what God has said, HIS WORD GOES INSIDE YOUR HEART. And your heart will help you love like God.

If you would like God, your heavenly Father to help you to know Him and the Words He has said, you can pray and say these words after me, or you can pray to God in your own words. Ready. Let's pray!

PRAYER

Father,
(Pause for Children to Repeat)
I want to know You
(Pause)
Will you help me?
(Pause)
I want to hear and believe You
(Pause)
Will You teach me to say
(Pause)
what You have said every day?
(Pause)
Thank You Father!
(Pause)
Will you help me
(Pause)
to think about Your Word?
(Pause)
Thank You Father!
(Pause)
Will You let Your Word
(Pause)
change my heart
(Pause)
so I will love like You?
(Pause)
Thank You for hearing me
(Pause)
and answering my prayer!
(Pause)
I love You!
(Pause)
Amen.

LEARNING SCRIPTURES FOR OUR BOOKS

INSTRUCTIONS:

1) Does anyone have something good to tell us that God did for you from His Word? (Listen to the testimonies of the children)

2) We are going to add a new scripture to our What Did God Say books?

3) Show children the Lesson 4 Scripture and let children know these are some Words God said.

4) Our new scripture is: "Don't let evil defeat you, but defeat evil by doing good."

5) What do you think God means when He says to you "Don't let evil defeat you, but defeat evil by doing good"? (Listen to responses)

6) God's way of doing things is different than how people in the world do things. God wants His children to do things like Him, in love. Father wants you to FORGIVE and to be kind and pray for people who act mean or evil. When you show love and kindness to someone who acts evil, you did not let the evil defeat or beat you! But when you do good things and show love, you will beat up and defeat the evil with good. That is God's way. In God's Kingdom, His children defeat evil by choosing to do good!

7) Let's say it boldly together: "Don't let evil defeat you, (pause) but defeat evil by doing good."

8) Let's say it again: "Don't let evil defeat you, (pause) but defeat evil by doing good."

9) Do you remember the name of the awesome love that Father has for you and everyone? (Listen to responses)

10) Your Father in heaven loves with a love that is not like the love on earth. His love is called agape love. Agape love is a heavenly amazing love. Father wants everyone to know His love so He wants you to be an ambassador for Jesus and show others God's kind of love.

11) Repeat after me. I am an ambassador for Jesus, (pause) and I choose to defeat evil (pause) by doing good.

12) Has anyone ever been mean or evil to you? (Listen to responses)

13) Can you think of some good things that you can do to defeat the evil? (Listen to responses and give feedback as appropriate)

14) Let's say the scripture together again. Don't let evil defeat you, (pause) but defeat evil (pause) by doing good. (repeat)

15) Ask children to take out their books. (CHILDREN WHO DID NOT BRING THEIR NOTE BOOKS, let them write their scripture on paper. Tell them to put it in their book when they get home.) (Provide notebooks for new children or make new book templates for this lesson.)

16) Write God's Words in your book.

17) Everyday declare or say God's Words so your ears can Hear His Words! You can read your book out loud so you can hear the words!

P.A.C.E.
www.ABC-Jesus.com
© All Rights Reserved

18) Every day pay attention and watch God do what He said because you believed Him, and you said what He said.

19) When you see God do what He said, write or draw a picture in your book about the good things God did for you.

20) And come tell us about it.

Let's Sing these Words God Said:
(Sing to the tune of "If you're happy and you know it")

**Don't let evil beat you, you beat it.
Don't let evil beat you, you beat it.
Don't let evil beat you, and this how you do it.
You beat up evil by do-ing good.**
(Repeat Several Times)

SONG: GOD LOVES ME!
(Sung to the tune of Barney Song)
(Do motions to Song)

YOU LOVE ME!
(Point upward, then to self)
I LOVE YOU!
(Point to self and upward)
YOU MAKE MY HEART GO PITTER-PAT!
(Point up, touch heart, Clap hands as you say pitter-pat)
YOU LOVED ME FIRST
(Point upward, then to self)
AND I LOVE YOU BACK!
(Kiss your hands and blow kisses up to Father)
YOU MAKE MY HEART GO PITTER-PAT!
(Point up, touch your heart, then clap hands as you say pitter-pat)
I LOVE YOU FATHER!
(Lift both hands up and SHOUT)

Scriptures:
Romans 12:21; Matthew 5:44-45; Matthew 6:14-15; John 20:22-23; Ephesians 4:32

FOLLOW UP ACTIVITY
CONSEQUENCES

Objectives to be Understood: We can receive good or bad consequences from the things we do.

Materials: Two Containers; Tape; Paper to write "OBEY" and "DISOBEY"; Consequence Cards; Scissors

Instructions:
1) Write and tape the word "Obey" on one container and the word "Disobey" on the other container.
2) Cut out the "Good" and "Bad" Consequence Cards. (Consequence Cards located at end of this activity) Put the "Good" Consequence Cards into the "Obey" container. Put the "Bad" Consequence Cards into the "Disobey" container.
3) Read Parent/Teacher Script

Parent/Teacher Script:
<u>Ask the children:</u> Have your parents ever told you to do something and you did not do it? *(Listen to Responses)*

What happened?
When you do something wrong, like disobey your parents, you could apologize for what you did, and your parents could forgive you, but there may still be a consequence. A consequence is the thing that happened after you did something good or bad.

Consequences could be good or bad. Remember God our Father has forgiven us and He has commanded all of us to forgive others also. But sometimes, even when others forgive us after we do wrong, we may still have consequences.

Let's play the Consequences game. Listen to this short situation. Then tell us what would you do?

SITUATION: You were playing ball and having a lot of fun. Your ball rolled into the middle of the street but your parents told you NOT to go into the street. No adult was around. What would you do?
(listen to responses)

Raise your hand if you would obey your parents and not go into the street. Raise your hand if you would go into the street and get your ball, and disobey your parents.
(For all the children who chose to obey their parents, congratulate them and have them pick from the OBEY container their good consequence.)

P.A.C.E.
www.ABC-Jesus.com
© All Rights Reserved

Situation (continued):

For the children who chose to disobey, have them pick from the DISOBEY can.
(Discuss how they feel with their consequences)

Remind the children that it is better to obey than to disobey. Ask the children who chose to disobey if they want to choose to obey their parents. If they say yes, let them pull from the OBEY container.
(Let the children know that God said in the bible)

"Children obey your parents in the Lord, for this is right."

Scriptures:
Ephesians 6:1-3; Colossians 3:13

P.A.C.E.
www.ABC-Jesus.com
© All Rights Reserved

BAD CONSEQUENCE CARDS
Cut on lines and put into "Disobey Container"

NO TV	Go to bed early	Hit by car
broken arm	Extra work to do – sweep the floor, wash the dishes	sit in chair in corner
Parents do not trust you	Cannot Play with Friends	You will receive a Spanking
You can NOT go to the beach	You can NOT go to the birthday party	No candy for you

GOOD CONSEQUENCE CARDS
Cut on lines and put into "Obey Container"

Receive Candy	Parents buy you a toy	You can go swimming
You can play ball	You can have fun with friends	You can go to the Beach
You can play games on the laptop	You can go to the birthday party	You can ride your bike
You can go roller skating	You can go to the amusement park	Your parents trust you

FOLLOW UP ACTIVITY
FORGIVING OTHERS

Objectives to be Understood: When you sin and ask for forgiveness God forgives you; but, if you do not forgive others God will not forgive you and ugly things like bitterness can go in your heart.

Materials: Rainbow Forgiving Hearts sheet (one per child); short strips of bright, colored, and white tissue paper; glue; black paper (could be tissue paper or another kind)

Activity: Parent/Teacher to make one "*Sample Rainbow Forgiving Heart*" before class time to show children and complete demonstration. (See Instructions to make Rainbow Sample Heart)

Parent/Teacher Script: When you do something bad and you pray and ask God to forgive you, does He forgive you?
(Listen to Responses)

Yes! The bible says, if we do something bad and we pray and ask God to forgive us that He forgives us every time and, He cleans our hearts with His love.
Do you know what Jesus said would happen if you DO NOT forgive others?
(Listen to responses)

Jesus said if we do not forgive others that God, our Father, will NOT forgive us.
God loves you so much. He knows that if you do not forgive others ugly things, like bitterness, can grow inside of your heart and make you think and act ugly.

Father wants you to be like Him and Jesus and forgive others like they forgave us. When Jesus died for our sins, He said, "Father forgive them for they know not what they do."

Even if the person did something really bad and hurt you, Jesus said to pray for them and God will help you to forgive them. God will take care of the entire situation when you do it His way. God's way to win *is -- when someone does evil or bad to you, YOU DO GOOD!* Forgiving others is good! Let's sing the <u>FORGIVE</u> Song.

FORGIVE SONG
(to tune of When Johnny comes marching home again)

**When someone does evil or bad to you;
Forgive! Forgive!
We'll do what Jesus told us to do;
Forgive! Forgive!
You may want to scream, you may want to shout;
But Father will make it all work out.
As we forgive each other, like Jesus told us to do.**

INSTRUCTIONS
Script: We are going to do an activity to show you what a heart that forgives and one that does not forgive may look like.

1) (Show the children your Sample rainbow Forgiving Heart).
2) Give each child a copy of the Forgiving Heart, some strips of white, bright, and colored tissue paper, and glue. (Do not give the black tissue paper at this time.)
3) Instruct each child to wad up the tissue paper and glue it inside of their Forgiving Heart paper.
4) After the child finishes, say something like: "These Forgiving Hearts look like happy rainbows that forgive others."
5) Instruct the children to put their Forgiving Heart in an area where the glue can dry.
6) (Place the Sample Rainbow Forgiving Heart where all children can see and reach.)
7) Show the children the black tissue paper, telling them "we are pretending this black paper is the ugly things that could grow in our hearts to make us think and act ugly when we do not forgive others."
8) Give each child a small wadded up piece of black (tissue) paper.
9) Instruct the children to put the black (tissue) paper on your Sample Rainbow Forgiving Heart.
10) After all the children have placed a black tissue paper on the heart, say: "Yuck! This heart is ugly and bitter because it did not forgive. (shake the black paper off of the Sample Rainbow Forgiving Heart.) (Ask Children) Are you going to forgive so you won't have an ugly bitter heart?" (Listen to responses) Let's all remember to forgive."
11) (Sing FORGIVE song again.) Ask parents to sing Forgive Song with their child.

Scriptures:
I John 1:9; Matthew 6:15; Matthew 5:44; Matthew 18:21-35; Romans 12:19-21; Luke 6:35; Luke 11:4

P.A.C.E.
www.ABC-Jesus.com
© All Rights Reserved

MY RAINBOW FORGIVING HEART

YOUR POWER IN JESUS

(Read Book 5)

PARENT LETTER 5

Dear Parents,
Please read and review with your child Story Lesson 5 entitled "Your Power in Jesus." In it we showed your child the power that Father has given them in Jesus. We want your child/ren to know that the truth of God's Word is found in the Holy Bible. Please encourage your child to read the Bible (on their age level), or if they cannot read, for someone to read to them.

Today our lesson showed your child their power to choose to change a bad thought to good. *(2 Corinthians 10:3-5)* We practiced changing a thought from one thing to another. The purpose was to show the children that they could control and change what they thought about by thinking of something else. This lesson also includes an exercise entitled "Truth or Lie." The purpose of the exercise is to help your child begin to recognize the truth of what their heavenly Father and Jesus has said about them, versus a lie of the enemy. *(John 8:44)* Please continue to help your child understand that some things that people say about them may not be true, but God's Word is true; and to always compare what others say to what God has said.

Your child also heard about the power that God has given them to choose to pray. *(Matthew 6:5-13)* The children heard some of the ways to enter the presence of heavenly Father in His throne room to get His help, and to pray in tongues. *(Hebrews 4:16; Romans 8:26-30; I Corinthians 14:2; Jude 1:20)* Please pray with them and remind him/her to pray every day and talk to heavenly Father.

Parents, we encourage you to make time daily to talk with your child about the things that concern him or her in their life by asking them relevant questions about their day and give Godly guidance. Pray with your child about their concerns, and remember to thank heavenly Father with them for the good things that He has done!

Sincerely yours in Christ Jesus,

Your Child's Teacher
Contact information: _____

FOLLOW UP ACTIVITIES

FOLLOW UP ACTIVITY
LEARNING GOD'S WORD

Objectives to be Understood:
1) Learn to think "new" like heavenly Father and Jesus by understanding God's Word, and
2) have fun learning God's Word.

Materials: Paper; Writing instrument, such as pencil, markers, pen; tape

INSTRUCTIONS:
1) Choose a scripture weekly (or more often as your family masters it).
2) Write the scripture out, and post it where your child and family members can see and read it.
3) Choose a specific time for the family to read or recite it by memory, such as before a meal. (Keep the atmosphere light so everyone wants to learn)
4) Engage in conversation to talk about the scripture and what it means during the meal. Here are a few examples to get you started with their personalized meanings in parenthesis:

   a. Galatians 3:26 - You are all children of God by believing in Christ Jesus. (I am God's child because I believe Jesus!)

   b. John 15:12- (Jesus said) Here is my command, Love each other, just as I have loved you. (Jesus loves me, and I love him, and others!)

   c. John 15:14 - (Jesus said) You are my friends if you do what I command. (I am a friend of Jesus because I obey Jesus!)

   d. I Corinthians 3:16 - Don't you know that you yourselves are God's temple? God's Spirit lives in you. (I am God's temple, and God's Holy Spirit lives in me!)

   e. Hebrews 4:16- So let us boldly approach the throne of grace. Then we will receive mercy. We will find grace to help us when we need it. (I can come boldly to God's throne and obtain help when I need it!)

   f. Colossians 2:10 - Because you belong to Christ, you have everything you need. He is the ruler over every power and authority. (I am complete in Christ Jesus!)

God bless you and your family! Continue to learn God's Word, understand it, pray, and trust your heavenly Father and Jesus to perform it. (Isaiah 55:11)

FOLLOW UP ACTIVITY
THE THRONE ROOM

Objectives to be Understood: For children to know: because of Jesus, you can confidently approach and pray to Father at His throne from which He gives mercy and grace to help you in time of need.

Materials: CD Player; CD of soft worship music

Parent/Teacher Script:
Father loves you so much that when Jesus returned to heaven Father made Jesus your High Priest. As your High Priest, Jesus speaks to Father to help you with things that you are to do on earth as a son or daughter of God. Jesus understands the things that you go through because He came to earth and was born as a baby and grew from a child to a man. Jesus has given you the right to come into Father's Throne Room anytime. In Father's Throne Room, He has a spiritual thing to give you called grace. Grace is God's favor on you. You are His favorite. He made no one else exactly like you. And He chose and picked you out to do a special work for Him on earth. This grace that God gives you is His heavenly power upon your heart that helps you to do all the things He planned for you. When you go in the throne room you can climb up on heavenly Father's lap and just love Him. Does anyone want to go into the throne room of Father?
(Listen to Responses
(Put on soft worship music, if available)

Say the words below to help the children think about their heavenly Father as the music plays:

With a pure heart, let's go to the throne and see our Father!
You can close your eyes.
Think about Father and His love.
See Him in your mind.
Now talk softly to Him, or sing to Him.
Tell Him how good He is.
Tell Him what is in your heart.
Thank Him! Thank Him for sending Jesus.
Be quiet and listen to what He says to you inside of your heart.
Receive His grace.
You are His child.
Pray. Talk to your Father now!
He's listening.
Remember to Thank Him.

Scriptures:
Hebrews 4:14-16; Hebrews 5:5-6; Ephesians 1:4-5; Matthew 5:8; I Thessalonians 5:17-18; I John 5:14-15; John 14:12-14 Hebrews 4:15-16

P.A.C.E.
www.ABC-Jesus.com
© All Rights Reserved

FOLLOW UP ACTIVITY
THE POWER IN YOUR WORDS

Objectives to be Understood: For children to know: that their Words contain the power of death and life in them.

Materials: Follow up Activity from Lesson 2 entitled "Tell Me Something Good."

Parent/Teacher Script:
Do you know your words have spirit power in them? *(Listen to responses)*
Say with me, "My words have spirit power." *(Encourage children to say with you)*
Your words make a difference for good or for bad. Your words can cause people to think something or not think something. Your words cause people to do something or *not* do something.
Let's play Red Light, Green Light. After we play we will talk about what happened with words.

The rules are:
- Choose someone as the SPEAKER – to call out the words, "Red light" or "Green light."
- All players (except speaker) line up next to each other (such as next to a wall).
- The goal is to get to the "HOME spot" (The HOME spot is a place you pick, such as a wall on the opposite side of the room, or if outside a certain tree, fence, etc.)
- When the speaker says RED LIGHT--all players STOP and FREEZE immediately. When the speaker says GREEN LIGHT—WALK FAST toward the HOME spot. The first one to get to the "HOME spot" wins.

(Play Game)
(After the Game, say the Parent/Teacher Script below)

Parent/Teacher Script:
Mostly every time you heard the speaker say Red Light, you stopped. When you heard Green Light you walked fast or you ran.

Your words tell people what you want them to do and what you don't want them to do. God said that the power of death and life are in your tongue. What do you think that means?
(Listen to Responses)

God put the *Spirit Power* of death and life in our words. Our tongues help words come out of our mouths. That is why the power of death and life is in our tongue.
God gave us the power to use our words for good or bad.

The devil is a liar who wants to kill us. He tries to make us say and do bad things. He wants to take the *spirit power* in our words and add a lie to it so the lies will pile up in our hearts.

Parent/Teacher Script (continued):

When we believe a lie that someone said about us or that the devil has whispered to our mind, it causes ugly things to grow in our heart. When ugly things get in our heart, we say bad things to others.

You can hurt people with the bad things you say. Or you can help people heal and get better with the good things you say.

God has said good things about His children! When we say God's good words, those words go into the heart and cause life to grow. When we used our words to play the Red light/Green light game, we had good fun!

Do you like to hear the good things our heavenly Father said about you? *(Listen to Responses)* God said He made you to be like Him! *That* is a good thing! Jesus and Father made us to be good!

Let's practice saying good things to each other.
Play: "Tell Me Something Good" game. *(See Lesson 2 Follow Up Activity)*

Scriptures:
Proverbs 18:21; Proverbs 12:18; Psalm 39:1; Proverbs 15:4; Proverbs 21:23; James 3:5; Genesis 1:26-28

FOLLOW UP ACTIVITY
WHAT DID GOD SAY? LESSON 5

Objectives to be Understood: For children to know:
1) God made you to be like Him
2) God's Word is alive and true
3) God's Word is like a sword
4) God's Word has the power of life in it, and
5) to say what God has said.

Activity: Children will write in their books the Scriptures/Words God Said.

Important Note: This activity is included in each of our 6 lessons with a different scripture in each lesson for children to receive into their hearts.

Materials: Pencils; Markers; Stapler; Pre-made book template or purchased notebooks (see Preparation below)

Preparation: To MAKE A BOOK
Pre-make book templates for each child by folding two sheets of paper in half and stapling (two staples on the folded side so pages open like a book); OR purchase lined notebooks.

Write out and post (where children can easily see) the following scripture:

DEATH AND LIFE ARE IN THE POWER OF THE TONGUE; AND THOSE WHO LOVE IT WILL EAT ITS FRUIT
Proverbs 18:21

REVIEW:

Parent/Teacher Script:
What does the power in God's Word do?
(Listen to responses)

The POWER in God's Words is sharp and cuts like a big SWORD. God's Word changes things to life and good when you believe Him.

Did you know that God gave you power in the Words you speak also?
(Listen to responses)

God put power in your tongue for you to speak Words that give life like He does.
The Bible has stories about God, and His power and how people who believed God used their power for good. The Bible tells you many things about God and yourself to help you to choose to live the way God planned for you.

TO KNOW GOD'S WORD

First, you must LET YOUR EARS HEAR GOD'S WORD AND BELIEVE IT.
Second, LET YOUR MOUTH SAY THE WORDS THAT GOD HAS SAID.
Third, Tell your mind to THINK ABOUT WHAT GOD HAS SAID.
When you think about what God has said, HIS WORD GOES INSIDE YOUR HEART. And your heart will help you love like God.

If you would like God, your heavenly Father to help you to know Him and the Words He has said, you can pray and say these words after me, or you can pray to God in your own words. Ready. Let's pray!

PRAYER

Father,
(Pause for Children to Repeat)
I want to know You
(Pause)
Will you help me?
(Pause)
I want to hear and believe You
(Pause)
Will You teach me to say
(Pause)
what You have said every day?
(Pause)
Thank You Father!
(Pause)
Will you help me
(Pause)
to think about Your Word?
(Pause)
Thank You Father!
(Pause)
Will You let Your Word
(Pause)
change my heart
(Pause)
so I will love like You?
(Pause)
Thank You for hearing me
(Pause)
and answering my prayer!
(Pause)
I love You!
(Pause)
Amen.

LEARNING SCRIPTURES FOR OUR BOOKS

Parent/Teacher Script:
Does anyone have something good to tell us that God did for you from His Word?
(Listen to the testimonies of the children)

We are going to add a new scripture to our What Did God Say books?
(Show children the Lesson 5 Scripture and let children know these are some Words God said.)

Our new scripture is in the Bible book of Proverbs 18:21. It says **Death and Life are in the power of the tongue and those who love it will eat its fruit.**
What do you think God meant when He said, Death and Life are in the power of the tongue and those who love it will eat its fruit?
(Listen to Responses)

Do you know why God put power in your tongue and the words you speak?
(Listen to Responses)

He made us to be like Him. When Father created the earth, He put everything on it to make it ready for His children. Father made us to be His family so that we would rule and make the whole earth good. He planned for His children to speak words that bring life. And that life would be all over the earth. So each person has the power that God gave them to speak things that are good and bring life, or things that are evil and bring death.
Why do you think the devil has power on the earth?
(Listen to Responses)

He gets power from bad and evil words spoken by people who don't understand that their evil words carry death in them. Many people wonder why their life is terrible when they speak words that go against God's good words.

This is why God told us that He made us with the power of death and life in our tongue and the words that we speak. And whatever words you are saying you will eat the fruit of the words you love to say. The fruit from the good words will bring life to you and others, but the fruit from the bad words spoken will bring death.

Let's say it boldly together:
Death and life (pause)
are in the power of the tongue; (pause)
and those who love it (pause)
will eat its fruit. Let's say it again.
(Repeat)

Have you ever had someone to tell you they love you?
(Listen to responses)

Parent/Teacher Script (continued):

Your Father in heaven loves you with a love that is not like the love on earth.
What is the name of the love that Father loves you with?
(Listen to responses)

His love is called agape love. Agape love is a heavenly amazing love.

Repeat after me!
God loves me (pause)
and His Word tells me (pause)
to say good things (pause)
and speak life, (pause)
like Father and Jesus.

Ask children to take out their books.
(CHILDREN WHO DID NOT BRING THEIR NOTE BOOKS, let them write their scripture on paper. Tell them to put it in their book when they get home.)
(Provide notebooks for new children or make new book templates for this lesson.)

Write God's Words in your book.
You can read your book out loud and everyday declare or say God's Words so your ears can Hear His Words!

Every day pay attention and watch God do what He said because you believed Him, and you said what He said.

When you see that God has done what He said, write or draw a picture in your book about the good things God did for you.
And come tell us about it.

Let's Sing these Words God Said:
(Sing to the tune of "If you're happy and you know it")

Death and life are in the power of the tongue.
Death and life are in the power of the tongue.
Death and life are in the power
Death and life are in the power
Death and life are in the power of the tongue.
(DECLARE!)
And you'll eat its fruit!
(Repeat Several Times)

SONG: GOD LOVES ME!

(Sung to the tune of Barney Song)
(Do motions to Song)

YOU LOVE ME!
(Point upward, then to self)

I LOVE YOU!
(Point to self and upward)

YOU MAKE MY HEART GO PITTER-PAT!
(Point up, touch heart, Clap hands as you say pitter-pat)

YOU LOVED ME FIRST
(Point upward, then to self)

AND I LOVE YOU BACK!
(Kiss your hands and blow kisses up to Father)

YOU MAKE MY HEART GO PITTER-PAT!
(Point up, touch your heart, then clap hands as you say pitter-pat)

I LOVE YOU FATHER!
(Lift both hands up and SHOUT)

Scriptures:
Proverbs 18:21; Proverbs 17:27-28; Matthew 15:11; Matthew 15:17-20; Ezekiel 37:1-10

FOLLOW UP ACTIVITY
HOW TO CHANGE YOUR THOUGHTS

Objectives To Be Understood: You have the power to change your thoughts from bad to good; God's living Word has life and light in it and will remove the darkness of any lie or bad thought.

Materials: Bible; Copies of Activity "I can change a thought from bad to good"; Pencils; Markers; Crayons

Parent/Teacher Script:
God told us to "take every thought captive and make it obey the Messiah." The Messiah is Jesus. What do you think God means when He said to take every thought you have captive, and make it obey our Messiah Jesus?
(Listen to Responses)

God is good and does everything right. Father does not tell you to do something that He has not given you the power and ability to do. God has given you the power over your mind and your thoughts. You have the power to change what you are thinking about from one thought to another. You can change a bad thought to something good.

One way to change something you don't want to think about is to sing a song out loud, or inside of your mind. Let's practice changing something you are thinking about from one thing to another.

Imagine and think about a big juicy red apple. The apple smells real good and you want to take a bite of it. Hmmm! You can almost taste it. Are you thinking about the apple?
(Listen to Responses)

Now quit thinking about the apple and think about how much Jesus loves you. Let's sing, Yes, Jesus loves me out loud.
(Sing song aloud together)

Next sing it silently inside of your mind so no one can hear.
(Sing song silently)

Were you able to think about the apple when you were singing and thinking about the song?
(Listen to Responses)

It's hard to think two thoughts at one time. So when you are thinking a bad thought, just change what you are thinking about to something good.

Parent/Teacher Script (continued):

God told us to think about things that are lovely, kind, good and true. God's Word is living and full of light that is lovely, kind, good and true. God's living Word is greater and more powerful than the darkness of any bad thought. Here are some living words full of light to think about and chase away dark, bad thoughts.

Jesus said, "I leave you peace. It is my own peace I give you. I give you peace in a different way than the world does. So don't be troubled. Don't be afraid."

Let's think about these words. Jesus is giving you His peace. Reach out and receive it. Take the peace of Jesus in your hands. Do you have it? Let the peace of Jesus fall all over you. His peace is not like the world's peace. His peace is flowing into every part of you. The peace of Jesus keeps your heart from worry. His peace surrounds you with angels to help you. Feel His peace, and know that you do not have to be afraid. Jesus and Holy Spirit are with you. You have the peace of Jesus. Think about it and say,

"I have the peace of Jesus."

Here's another living word of God to think about to make a bad thought leave:
"Don't worry about anything, but pray and ask God for everything you need, always giving thanks for what you have. And because you belong to Christ Jesus, God's peace will stand guard over all your thoughts and feelings. His peace can do this far better than our human minds."

Let's pray. Let's ask Father to help us remember to not worry about anything, but to pray and ask for His help, and to always thank Him.

Father,
You told me not to worry about anything.
You told me to ask you for everything I need.
Please remind me to always ask you to help me.
Thank you Father.
Amen.

Directions:
1) Give each child an "I can change a thought from bad to good "sheet, pencils, markers, and crayons.
2) Instruct children on how to complete the sheet. (See instructions on the sheet)
3) After the children complete their drawings, ask who wants to show their picture and tell about it.

Scriptures:
2 Corinthians 10:5; Isaiah 45:19; 2 Timothy 1:7; John 14:27; Philippians 4:6-8;
John 1:4-5; I John 1:5; I John 5:14-15; Romans 5:20

P.A.C.E.
www.ABC-Jesus.com
© All Rights Reserved

ACTIVITY: I CAN CHANGE A THOUGHT FROM BAD TO GOOD!

I can draw something I thought about that was BAD.

I can change that bad thought and draw something GOOD.

FOLLOW UP ACTIVITY
WHY THE DEVIL DOES NOT WANT YOU TO PRAY IN TONGUES!

Objectives to be Understood: When you pray in tongues you pray directly to God.

Materials: Paper, pencil, crayons, markers

Activity: Children can practice praying in tongues. Children can draw a picture of a secret place where they can pray in tongues or in their language to talk to Father in heaven.

Parent/Teacher Script: When Adam and Eve were first in the Garden of Eden, they believed their Father. They were His children. God would walk and talk with Adam and Eve in the Garden. When you believed Father and Jesus, you also became a child of God, to walk and talk with God, your Father every day.

When Jesus was on earth many people still did not believe him and said and did bad things. Since Father gave the world to His children He wants you, His child, to learn to say and do things His way. So Father sent from Himself and Jesus, Holy Spirit, to live in you and give you advice and help you do things God's right way.

Father even gave you a special way to pray in the Spirit. When you pray in the Spirit, Holy Spirit helps you to pray the language of God called tongues. When you pray in the Spirit or tongues you pray directly to Father all the good things He wants to happen on earth for you and others. When you pray in tongues Father and Jesus can command His angels to do it. When you pray in tongues, you can make good things happen on earth like in heaven. The devil does not like that. He doesn't want you to pray God's language. He does not want you to pray what Father wants. But we don't listen to the devil. We are Father's children! So let's pray in tongues now and make that old evil one run away fast!
(Those who want to pray in tongues, can do so now.)

Jesus told us to pray to our heavenly Father in a secret place. Your secret place is a quiet place where you can go to be alone and talk to God your Father by yourself.

Why do you think your heavenly Father wants you to pray to Him in a secret place?
(Listen to answers)

Your Father wants you to know He loves you. When you think about Him and spend time with Him in prayer in a secret place, God shows you His love openly. When you do not know what to pray to Father, just pray in the Sprit in tongues. It is the perfect prayer, or; you can pray and talk to your Father in your own language.

Activity:
1) Ask the children: Do you know any place in your house where you can go to be alone and pray to your heavenly Father? (Listen to answers) (Give some suggestions, such as, your bedroom and close the door, the bathroom).

2) Give each child a sheet of paper, pencil, crayons and markers.

3) Tell the children to pick a secret place in their home to pray to heavenly Father.

4) Tell children to draw a picture of the secret place they chose.

5) Remind children, it is special when they talk to their heavenly Father in their secret place. They can also talk to Father any place, any time.

Scriptures:
I Corinthians 14:2; Matthew 6:6; Ephesians 6:18; Romans 8:26-27; Jude 1:20

THE KINGDOM OF GOD

(Read Book 6)

PARENT LETTER 6

Dear Parents,
Please review today's topic, the Kingdom of God. The lesson focused on God's kingdom of love. It described heaven and some of the things the bible has said are there. Your child heard how Jesus showed love by healing the sick, raising the dead, making demons leave people, and telling people about his Father's kingdom of love. Your child heard that when they believe Jesus, he gave them the right to use his name to do what he did and greater things.
(John 14:12; Mark16:15-18)

We ask that you review the scripture of John 14:12-14 with your child to help him/her understand that Jesus truly gave them the right to use his name. Jesus said, "Most assuredly I say to you, he who believes in me, the works that I do he will do also, and greater than these he will do, because I go to my Father. And whatever you ask in my name, that I will do, that the Father may be glorified in the Son. If you ask anything in my name, I will do it."

Our story also described how Jesus gave his Father glory and honor. Let your child/ren know that they can also give heavenly Father glory like Jesus when they choose to love others. Please let your child know that when they believed Jesus, the Holy Spirit of love went into their heart and they received God's kingdom of love inside of them to show love to others.
(Luke 17:20-21; John 14:16-17)

What an awesome thing! Here's a song to sing with your child to help them remember to trust God and be led by Holy Spirit to love others.

(Sing to the tune of London Bridge is Falling down)

**Holy Spirit helps me love, helps me love, helps me love.
Holy Spirit helps me love, Because I obey Je-sus!**

Sincerely yours in Christ Jesus,

Your Child's Teacher
Contact information: _____

FOLLOW UP ACTIVITIES

FOLLOW UP ACTIVITY
A SONG ABOUT LOVE!

Objectives to be Understood: You can give Father glory when you sing and declare the truth of His love and show others His love.

Materials: None

Instructions:

Let's sing a song about love.

(Point to yourself and say)
I have love inside of me.

(Now hold your hands up)
It's growing BIG just like a tree.

(Frame hands around your eyes)
Watch all the things God does through me,

(Point to yourself and say)
Cause I have love inside of me.

FOLLOW UP ACTIVITY
MY BOOK OF LOVE TO GIVE FATHER GLORY!

Objectives to be Understood: You can give Father glory when you think about ways to help others and show them His love.

Materials: *Copy of book pattern, markers, crayons, pencils, stapler, scissors*

Instructions: Give each child a book pattern and materials. For young children that cannot read yet, instruct them to draw a picture of how they will show love; and older children can write what they will do and/or draw a picture. Encourage children to tell about their books. Help younger children read words and cut out pattern as needed.

Parent/Teacher Script:
Draw a picture or write in your book, what you will do to show love, because showing love gives heavenly Father glory, in Jesus.

Scriptures:
John 13:31-35; John 14:13-15; John 17:4-10

I will show Love to a New Student at School.

8.

My Book of Love!

Written by

I will show Love to Someone who was Mean.

6.

I will show Love to Someone Sick.

3.

I will show Love to someone Hungry. 2.	**I will show Love to an Older Person.** 7.
I will show Love to My Parents. 4.	**I will show Love to My Brother, Sister or Friend.** 5.

FOLLOW UP ACTIVITY
WHAT DID GOD SAY? *LESSON 6*

Objectives to be Understood: For children to know:
1) God made you to be like Him;
2) God's Word is alive and true;
3) God's Word is like a sword;
4) God's Word has the power of life in it, and;
5) to say what God has said.

ACTIVITY: Children will write in their books the Scriptures/Words God Said.

IMPORTANT NOTE: This activity is included in each of our 6 lessons with a different scripture in each lesson for children to receive into their hearts.

MATERIALS: Pencils; Markers; Stapler; Pre-made book template or purchased notebooks (see Preparation below)

Preparation: To MAKE A BOOK
Pre-make book templates for each child by folding two sheets of paper in half and stapling (two staples on the folded side so pages open like a book); OR purchase lined notebooks.

Write out and post (where children can easily see) the following scripture:

…HE WHO BELIEVES IN ME, THE WORKS THAT I DO HE WILL DO ALSO; AND GREATER (WORKS) THAN THESE HE WILL DO, BECAUSE I GO TO MY FATHER.
John 14:12

Review:

1) Do you know who God made you to be like? (Listen to responses)

   Answer: God made you to be like Him, say good words that give life and love others.

2) Why did Father call Jesus The Word?

   Answer: Jesus obeyed His Father and always did what His Father said so Father called Jesus The Word.

3) Different writers wrote what God told them to write in the Bible. What are the words in the Bible called? Answer: The Words in the Bible are called scriptures.

4) What are the different parts of the Bible called? Answer: The Bible has different parts called books. The scripture that we will learn today can be found in the book of John the fourteenth chapter and the 12th verse. John 14:12

   The Bible tells us what Jesus said about the Kingdom of heaven, and the power Jesus has given to you in His name to do good works on earth as it is in heaven.

TO KNOW GOD'S WORD

First, you must LET YOUR EARS HEAR GOD'S WORD AND BELIEVE IT.
Second, LET YOUR MOUTH SAY THE WORDS THAT GOD HAS SAID.
Third, Tell your mind to THINK ABOUT WHAT GOD HAS SAID.
When you think about what God has said, HIS WORD GOES INSIDE YOUR HEART. And your heart will help you love like God.

If you would like God, your heavenly Father to help you to know Him and the Words He has said, you can pray and say these words after me, or you can pray to God in your own words. Ready. Let's pray!

PRAYER

Father,
(Pause for Children to Repeat)
I want to know You
(Pause)
Will you help me?
(Pause)
I want to hear and believe You
(Pause)
Will You teach me to say
(Pause)
what You have said every day?
(Pause)
Thank You Father!
(Pause)
Will you help me
(Pause)
to think about Your Word?
(Pause)
Thank You Father!
(Pause)
Will You let Your Word
(Pause)
change my heart
(Pause)
so I will love like You?
(Pause)
Thank You for hearing me
(Pause)
and answering my prayer!
(Pause)
I love You!
(Pause)
Amen.

LEARNING SCRIPTURES FOR OUR BOOKS

Instructions:
1) Does anyone have something good to tell us that God did for you? (Listen to the testimonies of the children)
2) We are going to add a new scripture to our What Did God Say books?
3) Show children the Lesson 6 Scripture and let children know these are some Words God said.
4) Our new scripture is: Jesus said, "He who believes in Me, the works that I do he will do also, and greater works than these he will do, because I go to My Father."
5) What do you think Jesus means when He said, He who believes in Jesus, the works that Jesus do you will do also, and greater works than these you will do, because He goes to His Father?
6) What are some of the good works that Jesus did on earth to show people Father's kingdom of love?

    Answer: Jesus told people about Father's Kingdom of love. Jesus healed the sick. He made dead people's spirit come back into their bodies. Jesus made the devil and demons leave and quit hurting people.

7) Why do you think Jesus showed God's children on earth what the Kingdom of Heaven is like?

    Answer: Father has a plan. His children were to rule earth the same way that He ruled heaven, in love. But earth was not like heaven anymore. So Jesus showed God's children on earth what love looked like. Love is kind, good and helps others.

8) Jesus said when we believe Him, the works that He do we will do also, and we can do greater works than these, because He is with His Father God.
9) Let's say it boldly together: Jesus said, (PAUSE) He who believes in me (PAUSE) the works that I do (PAUSE) he will do also; (PAUSE) and greater than these (PAUSE) he will do (PAUSE) because I go to My Father. Let's say it again. (Repeat)
10) Have you ever had someone to tell you they love you? (Listen to responses)
11) Your Father in heaven loves you with a love that is not like the love on earth. His love is called agape love. Agape love is a heavenly amazing love. Repeat after me. God loves me, (pause) and because I believe Jesus (pause) God has given me power (pause) in the name of Jesus (pause) to show His Kingdom (pause) to heal the sick, (pause) raise the dead, (pause) make demons leave, (pause) and tell people that Jesus loves them.

12) Ask children to take out their books. (CHILDREN WHO DID NOT BRING THEIR NOTE BOOKS, let them write the scripture (the words of John 14:12) on paper. Tell them to put it in their book when they get home.) (Provide notebooks for new children or make new book templates for this lesson.)

13) Write God's Words in your book.

14) Everyday declare or say God's Words so your ears can Hear His Words! You can read your book out loud so you can hear the words!

15) Every day pay attention and watch God do what He said because you believed Him, and you said what He said.

16) When you see God do what He said, write or draw a picture in your book about the good things God did for you. And come tell us about it.

Let's Sing these Words God Said:
(Sing to the tune of "If you're happy and you know it")

**I will do the works that Je-sus does.
I will do the works that Je-sus does.
Yes, I believe He's true.
And greater works I'll do.
Because I believe that Jesus Christ is true!**
(Repeat Several Times)

SONG: GOD LOVES ME!
(Sung to the tune of Barney Song)
(Do motions to Song)
YOU LOVE ME!
(Point upward, then to self)
I LOVE YOU!
(Point to self and upward)
YOU MAKE MY HEART GO PITTER-PAT!
(Point up, touch heart, Clap hands as you say pitter-pat)
YOU LOVED ME FIRST
(Point upward, then to self)
AND I LOVE YOU BACK!
(Kiss your hands and blow kisses up to Father)
YOU MAKE MY HEART GO PITTER-PAT!
(Point up, touch your heart, then clap hands as you say pitter-pat)
I LOVE YOU FATHER!
(Lift both hands up and SHOUT)

Scriptures:
John 14:12; Mark 16:15-18; Matthew 10:7-10; Luke 9:1; Matthew 28:18-20

FOLLOW UP ACTIVITY
MY PRAYER BAG

Objectives to be Understood: To pray for things important to God; you can pray for others; and, when you pray with a friend who agrees with you, it is powerful.

Materials: Prepare a basket entitled "Some of the Things Father Wants You to Pray For." Place strips of paper in the basket with the following topics:
- Pray for others.
- Give thanks for others.
- Pray for yourself and that you want to obey Father.
- Pray and give Father all of your cares and anything that makes you afraid or angry.
- Pray for your leaders and those in charge of things.
- Pray for the peace of Jerusalem, God's holy city on earth.
- Pray for people who are mean or who have hurt you or someone else.
- Pray that Father's children go and tell others about Jesus and show others what God's Kingdom is like. (heal the sick, raise the dead, cast out demons)

Parent/Teacher Script:
God told us who to pray for. We are to first of all make heartfelt, humble and sincere requests, prayers and give thanks for all others. He tells us to think about His love and ask for what we want. Pray for others. He wants you to give Him all your worries because He cares for you. We are told to pray for our leaders, those who are in charge of things. We are commanded to pray for the peace of Jerusalem (God's holy city on earth). Jesus commanded us to pray for those who are mean to you and who mistreat you. That is what Jesus did. He prayed for those who mistreated Him and who did not know His Father.

Jesus also prayed for Himself. He prayed for God's will to be done regarding Him going to the cross. Father answered Jesus prayer and sent an angel to strengthen Him. Jesus said to pray that workers be sent to show and tell the people about God's Kingdom. Workers are God's children and ambassadors.

How will you know that God heard your prayer?
(Listen to answers)

God said in His Word, that **If** we ask for anything according to His will, He hears us. And if we know He hear us, whatever we asked, we know that we have what we asked for. We have to pray according to God's will, and His will is "love."

Parent/Teacher Script (continued):

Did you know that Jesus said, if two of you on earth agree on anything you pray for, that Father in heaven will do what you ask? This is also a way that you can pray --- with a friend, who agrees with you about what you are asking of Father. Two of you can pray to Father for someone who needs help or for anything on your hearts.

Prayer Activity:
1) Give each child a paper bag to decorate as their PRAYER BAG.
2) Tell the children to write the names of people they will pray for and place in the bag. Whenever they think of others to pray for they can add them to their Prayer Bag. Remind the children to thank Father because He will answer their prayers.
3) Encourage children to put their Prayer Bags aside to take home later.
4) Pair children to pray together.
5) Remind children that they will pull from the basket something God wants them to pray about.
6) Let one child from each pair select a prayer slip from the basket.
7) Encourage children to pray together and talk to Father about what is on the prayer slip of paper.
8) Thank children for obeying Father and praying for the things He said.

Scriptures:
I Timothy 2:1-2; I Peter 5:7; Psalm 122:6; Matthew 5:44; Luke 23:34; Luke 22:41-43; Matthew 9:36-38; Matthew 18:19; I John 5:14-15

P.A.C.E.
www.ABC-Jesus.com
© All Rights Reserved

FOLLOW UP ACTIVITY
DON'T BE AFRAID!

Objectives to be Understood: You don't have to be afraid. You can pray and use the power and authority in Jesus name to do what He did and greater.

Materials: Copies of the "Ask me to Pray for You" cards; scissors; glitter stickers; puppet or baby doll

Activity: Children will decorate their "Ask me to Pray for you" Cards and role play using their authority and power in Jesus.

Parent/Teacher Script:
Have you ever been afraid of something?
(listen to responses)

What were you afraid of?
(listen to responses)

Jesus gave us power over ALL the power of the enemy and He said nothing shall by any means hurt you.

Did you know that Jesus told us, Do NOT be afraid and to only believe Him? Jesus will never leave you.

Do you believe Jesus?
(Listen to responses)

Do you love Jesus?
(Listen to responses)

Jesus said when you love Him you will obey Him, and anything you ask the Father for in His name, He will do it.

God, our Father in heaven put power in the name of Jesus. You do not have to be afraid when you pray to our Father, in Jesus name.

You can pray to Father and make demons and scary things leave. After you pray to Father, YOU speak to it and tell it to GET OUT, IN JESUS NAME! It has to go because Jesus said He would do it! Jesus loves you!

You can pray and ask Father to make a sick person get well. After you pray, YOU speak to the sickness and tell the Sickness to LEAVE THEIR BODY, IN JESUS NAME! Can you do that? You will each get 2 "Ask me to Pray for You" cards to give to two people that you want to pray for God to help them.

Parent/Teacher Script (continued):

After we decorate our cards we are going to pretend this puppet is afraid of the dark so you can practice praying to Father and tell the scary thing in its room to "LEAVE AND NEVER COME BACK, IN JESUS NAME!"

We will also pretend the puppet is sick so you can pray to Father in Jesus name, and command the sickness to leave.

Let's decorate our "Ask me to Pray for You" cards.
1) Give each child 2 "Ask me to Pray for You" cards and jewel stickers to decorate the back side of the card that has no writing.

2) As the children decorate their cards, show them the puppet and tell them the puppet is afraid of being in a dark room. The puppet thinks scary things are in the room and he wants you to pray for him.

3) Ask children: Will you pray to Father in Jesus name and ask Him to use you to help make the scary things leave its room? (Guide children as needed) (Prayer Example: Father, will you help make the scary things leave its room, in Jesus name?)

4) Instruct the Children: Now use the power in Jesus name and YOU command the scary thing to leave his room. (Guide Children as needed) (Remind the children they do not have to scream or talk loud.) (Example: Scary thing, Leave! In Jesus name!)

5) Remember first, you pray to Father and ask Him for the help you need, in Jesus name. After you pray, you speak to it, and tell it what to do, in Jesus name. It has to obey the power in Jesus name.

Situation:
The puppet has a fever and feels sick and it wants you to pray for it to be well.

Will you pray to Father in Jesus name and ask Father to use you to heal the (puppet)? (Guide children as needed) (Example: Father, will you heal (the puppet) in Jesus name?

Now speak to the sickness and tell it to leave, in Jesus name!
(Example: Sickness leave! In Jesus name!)

Ask the children: Who should you pray to when you need help?
(Answer: We pray to Father in Jesus name)

After you pray and trust God, what do you do?
(Answer: We tell it what to do, in Jesus name.)

What will you do if you begin to get afraid of something?
(Listen to answers)

Pray and ask Father to help you NOT to be afraid, in Jesus name. You never have to be afraid again! You can always get the help you need from Father in Jesus name.

You made 2 "Ask Me to Pray for You" cards. Find someone to pray for. Ask them if you can pray for them. If they say yes, give them a card. Ask them, what do you want me to pray for? After they tell you, pray for them! When you pray, trust God, He will answer your prayer!

Scriptures:
Luke 8:50; John 14:27; Matthew 28:20(b); Luke 10:19; Mark 16:15-18; Philippians 2:9-10
John 14:12-14; John 14:21; Mark 11:22-24; Hebrews 4:15-16

Cut out Cards

Ask Me to Pray for You! **What do you want me to pray?**	**Ask Me to Pray for You!** **What do you want me to pray?**
Ask Me to Pray for You! What do you want me to pray?	**Ask Me to Pray for You!** What do you want me to pray?
Ask Me to Pray for You! What do you want me to pray?	**Ask Me to Pray for You!** What do you want me to pray?
Ask Me to Pray for You! What do you want me to pray?	**Ask Me to Pray for You!** What do you want me to pray?

FOLLOW UP ACTIVITY
SHOWING GOD'S KINGDOM

Objectives to be Understood: You can show God's Kingdom to others

Materials: Cell Phone Video Camera

Activity: To discuss and practice showing God's love and kindness

Parent/Teacher Script: A Kingdom is the entire place where a king has power to be in charge as the leader. When you were born again, Father put His Kingdom, His Holy Spirit, in you. In your spirit, Jesus made you a king and priest unto Him. Jesus made you His leader to show God's Kingdom of love to others. Since God our heavenly Father is love, the way you show His kingdom is to show others love like Father and Jesus. Love is an action of kindness. Many times you can see love and kindness. God, our Father showed His great love and kindness for us when He sent Jesus to die for us.

If _____ *(say a child's name)* asked for help and I said I would help *him/her*, am I being kind and showing love? (Listen to answers) But what if I did not do what I said? What if I never went to help *him/her*? Is that showing love or kindness?
(Listen to answers)

No, that is not showing love or kindness. How do you think _____ *(child's name)* would feel if I ignored *him/her* and did not do what I said?
(Listen to answers)

"*S/he* might feel bad." That is NOT showing God's kingdom and love.
What are some ways you can be kind and show love to another child or your sister or brother?
(Listen to answers)
(Suggestions: You could: be a friend and play nicely; no hitting, pushing, or yelling at them, you could listen when they talk to you, answer nicely, etc.)

How could you show love to your parents?
(Listen to answers)
(Suggestions: You could: obey them; be respectful by not talking rude to them; help them; listen to them)

Every time you show love and kindness, you are showing God's Kingdom. You are showing others how our Father does things in heaven. Holy Spirit can help you and remind you to show God's Kingdom. You can pray every day and ask our Father to help you show His Kingdom of love to others.

Let's pray.

**Father,
Will you help me show your Kingdom of love and be kind to others?
Thank you Father!
In Jesus name. Amen.**

ACTIVITY:
1) Script: We are going to pretend that one of you is a new child at school. All of the other children are playing. You see the new child who looks afraid. You decide to show kindness by being a friend to the new child. The Bible says in order to have friends, you must show yourself friendly. Think about what you would say to the new child. Don't tell us yet. You will get a chance to practice being friendly to say and do the kind things you are thinking about. We can record it on the cell phone. Afterwards we can watch it.
2) Choose someone to be the new child.
3) Choose someone to be the friend.
4) Record it on your cell phone as the children talk to each other.
5) Show the video recording to the children.
6) Repeat (numbers 2-4) until all children that want to participate have had a turn.

After everyone has had a turn, SAY:
"Good job! When you are kind, you show the Kingdom of God to others. Who remembers that the Bible said -- to have friends, you must show yourself to be what?
(listen to answers)

Friendly! (Repeat)

To have friends, you must show yourself to be
(pause for children to answer)

Friendly!"

The bible says there is a friend who sticks closer to you than a brother.
Who do you think that is?
(Listen to answers)

It's Jesus!

Scriptures:
Luke 17:21; Matthew 22:37-40; James 2:18-20; Revelation 1:6; Matthew 21:28-31; Proverbs 18:24

FOLLOW UP ACTIVITY
I HAVE A PURPOSE!

Objectives to be Understood: God has given you a purpose and will speak to you.

Materials: My Purpose Certificate; Pencils, decorative confetti, glue, paper

Activity: To write what God said on the certificate, decorate, and keep it

Parent/Teacher Script:
Your heavenly Father chose you! You need to understand that heavenly Father gave you a special thing to do for Him on earth. It's called your purpose. Father gave you everything you need to finish your purpose. Father told you to trust and have faith in Jesus. He gave you all blessings in your spirit. When you received Holy Spirit He gave you His kingdom to live in you. He made you different from everyone else. Nobody can do what God sent you to do, *like* you can. Do you want to know your purpose?
(Listen to answers)

Do you want to know why God sent you here? If you want to know, we can pray and ask our heavenly Father to tell you your purpose.
(Pray for each child individually)

SAY TO CHILD: Listen to what God is saying to you, then tell me what you hear Him say.
PRAY: FATHER, WILL YOU TELL _____HIS/HER PURPOSE?
(QUIETLY WAIT WHILE GOD SPEAKS TO THE CHILD'S HEART)

When the child tells you what they heard God say, repeat it back to the child, and write it on paper so the child may copy it.
- Celebrate with each child giving them a high five!
- THANK GOD and PRASE God with the child.
- (Let the child know) You can talk to God in prayer about anything.
- After God speaks to the child's heart: Give the child a MY PURPOSE certificate to decorate and write down what God said to them.

Scriptures:
Ephesians 1:3-5; Ephesians 1:9-11; Luke 17:21; Mark 11:22; Matthew 7:7-8; Ephesians 1:17-19; I John 5:14-15

MY PURPOSE

I PRAYED AND ASKED GOD MY PURPOSE AND THIS IS WHAT HE SAID

Name

Date

P.A.C.E.
www.ABC-Jesus.com
© All Rights Reserved

SONGS FOR YOU TO SING WITH CHILDREN

THE PRAYER SONG

(Sung to the tune of Up on the Housetop)

**Up in the heavens Jesus calls
Father loves you, one and all.
He sent Christ Jesus to tell you so,
Pray to the Father, He'll let you know.**
Chorus
**You can pray, do it today.
You can pray, do it today.
Pray to Father, He's waiting for you.
He will tell you what to do.**

I SAY I LOVE YOU FATHER

(Sung to the tune of Wee Willie Winkle runs through the town)

**I say I love you Father,
And this is what You said.
Every day, talk to Me.
Before you go to bed!**

**I pray and talk to Father.
He said that He would keep.
Everything safe for me
When I go to sleep!**

I CHOOSE GOD!

(Sung to the tune of Mary had a little lamb)

I choose God cause God loves me.
God loves me.
God loves me.
I choose God cause God loves me.
God loves me all day long.

With God's love I choose to sing.
Choose to sing.
Choose to sing.
With God's love I choose to sing.
I sing a happy song

I LOVE YOU JESUS

(Action Song to the tune and movements of The Hokey Pokey)

(children stand in circle to do this song)
You put your <u>right hand</u> in.
You take your <u>right hand</u> out.
You put your <u>right hand</u> in and you shake it all about.
You say I love You Jesus
And you turn yourself around.
(Clap!)
That's what it's all about.
(Shout!)
I LOVE YOU JESUS!
(Repeat: Each time replacing the word right hand for)
(left hand; right leg, left leg; head; Whole Self)
(Chorus)
You SAAY, I love You Jesus!
You SAAY, I love You Jesus!
You SAAY, I love You Jesus
(Clap!)
That's what it's all about.
(Shout!)
I LOVE YOU JESUS!

P.A.C.E.
www.ABC-Jesus.com
© All Rights Reserved

THANK YOU JESUS!

(Sung to the tune of I am Special)

(Extend your hands up and say)
Thank you Jesus! Thank you Jesus!
(Point to yourself and say)
God forgave me! God forgave me!
(Point upwards)
You took my sins upon you!
You took my sins upon you!
(Point to yourself and say)
Now I'm free! Now I'm free!

HOLY SPIRIT HELPS ME LOVE!

(Sing to the tune of London Bridge is falling down)

Holy Spirit helps me love,
Helps me love,
Helps me love.
Holy Spirit helps me love,
Because I obey Je-sus!

THE FRUIT OF THE SPIRIT SONG!

I have LOVE inside of me.
Do-Daw! Do-Daw!
It's growing BIG just like a tree. Because I show LOVE today!
OH, I'LL SHOW LOVE TODAY!
I'LL SHOW LOVE TODAY!
When I show LOVE it grows in me.
SO I'LL SHOW LOVE TODAY!
(Repeat: Each time replacing the word LOVE for a different Fruit of the Spirit)
(JOY; PEACE; PATIENCE; GENTLENESS; GOODNESS; FAITH; MEEKNESS; SELF-CONTROL)

A Song to lead Children into Thanksgiving/Worship

JESUS WILL NEVER LEAVE ME

(Sung to Tune of Yes, Jesus Loves Me)

Jesus loves me He's with me now.
He'll never leave me, No way! No How!
Father sent Jesus to set me free.
Jesus promised He would never leave me.
(Chorus)
Je-sus will never leave me.
Je-sus will never leave me.
Je-sus will never leave me.
That's why I thank God now!
Alleluia!
(Sing several times)
(Encourage children to thank God with words such as)
Thank your heavenly Father for sending Jesus!
Thank you Father!
Thank you Jesus!
(Sing again as Holy Spirit leads)

HOLY SPIRIT HELPS ME DO THINGS RIGHT

(Sung to Tune of London Bridge is Falling Down)

Holy Spirit helps me do things right.
Do things right
Do things right
Holy Spirit helps me do things right.
When I ask Him day or night.
I will practice with all my might
All my might
All my might
Holy Spirit helps me do things right
When I ask Him day or night.

P.A.C.E.
www.ABC-Jesus.com
© All Rights Reserved

GOOD THOUGHTS

(Say as an Action Poem. Make up your own motions)

**Bad thought, Bad thought,
I say No!
Bad thought, Bad thought,
Go! Go! Go!
Good thought, Good thought,
I say Come!
Thank You Jesus! It is done!**
(Ask questions after children learn the Action Poem.)
Can anyone tell us a good thought to think about?

THIS IS WHAT I CAN DO

(This is an Action Song Circle Game)
(To the tune of: This is what I can do!)

Instructions:
1) Have the children sit on floor in a circle.
2) All children say the words together.
3) At the end of the song, one lead child does some type of body movement to show what they can do, such as lifting their arms up and down, moving their head from side to side, etc.
4) All children do the same motions of the lead child.
5) Repeat until each child has had a turn.

**This is what I can do!
Jesus said that you can too!
This is what I can do!
It's his gift to me and you!**

I LOVE YOU

(Sung to the tune of the Barney Song)

I love you.
You love me.
We are in God's family.
I love you just like Jesus told me too.
Raise your hand and shout, I DO!
I DO!

JESUS IS HIS NAME

(Sung to tune of B. I. N. G. O.)

I have a friend who loves me BIG,
and Jesus is His name.
He told me to love others BIG.
to love them just the same.
J. E. S. U. S,
J. E. S. U. S,
J. E. S. U. S,
and Jesus is His name!

FORGIVE

(to tune of When Johnny comes marching home again)

When someone does evil or bad to you;
Forgive! Forgive!
We'll do what Jesus told us to do;
Forgive! Forgive!
You may want to scream, you may want to shout.
But Father will make it all work out.
As we forgive each other, like Jesus told us to do.

LISTEN

(A transition poem for children to do actions in readiness
for hearing a Foundation Curriculum Story or a Bible Story teaching)

Eyes look up!
Eyes look down!
Eyes can search until you find!
Colors, Colors, all around!
Eyes find red.
(Look around and find something red)
Eyes find blue.
(Look around and find something blue)
Eyes find green.
(Look around and find something green)
And yellow too.
(Look around and find something yellow)
Raise your right hand to the sky.
Now raise your left hand way up high.
Put your hands together.
Good! You've made a pact.
Now gently place them in your lap.
And LISTEN,
as I read to you,
what Jesus told us all to do!
(Read Story to Children)

I CHOSE JESUS

(A Challenge Poem for each group to say their part to Jesus from their heart)

Instructions:
1) Instruct half of class to say first part of poem, for example, the words:" I Chose Jesus."
2) Tell other half of class to repeat second part of poem after you. For example, "Today He is mine!"
3) Continue until entire poem is said aloud.

>I Chose Jesus – Today He is mine!
>I Chose Jesus – I will thank Him all the time!
>I Chose Jesus – I'm Father's Child, it's true!
>I Chose Jesus – He teaches me what to do!
>I Chose Jesus – Because He loves me so!
>I Chose Jesus – Soon everyone will know!
>I Chose Jesus – Holy Spirit lives in me!
>I Chose Jesus –And everyone will see!

I RECEIVED HOLY SPIRIT

(A Challenge Poem for each group to say their part to Jesus from their heart)
(See Instructions above)

>I received Holy Spirit. -- God's gift to me was free.
>I received Holy Spirit. -- And now He lives in me.
>I received Holy Spirit. -- Jesus is my bread.
>I received Holy Spirit. -- And now I'm Spirit led.

JESUS IS MY SUPER HERO!

(Sung to the tune of Late last night when we were all in bed Old Lady Leary..)

**Jesus my Super Hero, He's always there for me!
The best Super Hero, He died and made me free!
Before He rose up from the grave, Jesus beat the devil down.
And one day He will put him in the ground, with FIRE, FIRE, FIRE!**

YES, MY FATHER LOVES ME!

(Sung to the tune of Itsy Bitsy Spider)

**Yes, my Father loves me! He doesn't tell me why.
He whispers and He tells me, I'm the apple of His eye!
I love Him! Yes, I love Him! And I will tell Him so!
I love You, my Father! I'll shout for all to know!
(SHOUT)
I LOVE YOU FATHER!**

JESUS IS MY FRIEND

(To the Tune of The Other Day I met a Bear)
*(Adult says line first. Children repeat line after adult.
Then adult and children say line together. See cues*)*

The other day	*(adult)
The other day	*(adult and children)
I met a friend	*(adult)
I met a friend	*(adult and children)
He is my friend	*(adult)
He is my friend	*(adult and children)
Through thick and thin	*(adult)
Through thick and thin	*(adult and children)
The other day I met a friend. He is my friend through thick and thin	*(adult and children)
He's with me now	*(adult)
He's with me now	*(adult and children)
He's in my heart	*(adult)
He's in my heart	*(adult and children)
He showed me love	*(adult)
He showed me love	*(adult and children)
Right from the start	*(adult)
Right from the start	*(adult and children)
He's with me now. He's in my heart. He showed me love right from the start.	*(adult and children)
Jesus His name	*(adult)
Jesus His name	*(adult and children)
He is my friend	*(adult)
He is my friend	*(adult and children)
He's with me now	*(adult)
He's with me now	*(adult and children)
Right to the end	*(adult)
Right to the end	*(adult and children)
Jesus His name. He is my friend. He's with me now right to the end.	*(adult and children)

GRACE

(Sung to tune of Old McDonald had a Farm)
(Teach this Grace Song to children to pray to God every day and whenever they are having a hard time)

**I need Your Grace right now Father,
Will you help me please?
I Thank You for Your Grace right now,
You gave me what I need.
So I thank you here, and I thank you there.
Here I thank. There I thank. Everywhere I thank You.
I Thank You for Your Grace Fa-ther,
You gave me what I need.**

CAN YOU PRAY TODAY?

(Sung to the tune of: Did you feed my cow? By Ella Jenkins)

Can you pray today?
Yes ma'am!
Can you tell me what to say?
Yes ma'am!
What do I say?
Thank you LORD!
Do you think that's good?
Yes ma'am!
Will Jesus say you should?
Yes ma'am!
How did you pray?
Just like this!
(Hands together in prayer position)
How did you pray?
Just like this!
(Hands together in prayer position)
Can you thank God twice?
Yes ma'am!
Thank you Lord!
Thank you Lord!
(Repeat)
Wasn't that nice?
Yes ma'am!
Wasn't that nice?
Yes ma'am!
Now you know what to do!
Yes ma'am!
Now you know what to do!
Yes ma'am!
When Jesus tells you to…
ALWAYS PRAY!
(Ask: Who wants to pray?)

APPENDIX

I HAVE THE CURRICULUM

NOW WHAT DO I DO?
AND
WHERE DO I BEGIN?

WITH PRESCHOOLERS
Ages 3 – 5 years old

P.A.C.E.
www.ABC-Jesus.com
© All Rights Reserved

Purpose: To plan activities that role-model and reinforce the Word and Love of God so children will see, hear, believe, understand and choose to live as children of God.

ROOM SET-UP

The areas that may be used in your room set up could include, tables and chairs, a circle area, and space for free choice centers. Improvise as needed. Use your outdoor space when you can. A brief description of suggestions for the use of the areas follows.

Tables and Chairs: to sit and do Follow-up Activities such as arts and crafts that reinforce the lesson; have snacks; play with table toys/board games; hear Bible stories; have conversations; sing songs; musical instruments; finger plays; review of day's activities, etc.

Circle: (to be seated or stand on carpeted floor area, if possible, or could place masking tape on floor in shape of circle) sing songs; do finger plays; introduction of day's activities; Foundation Curriculum story lesson; conversations; praise and worship; Bible verse; circle games; dance; introduce scripture on word wall; play musical instruments, etc.

Free Choice Center ideas (see Free Choice Centers)

Outdoors: use the outdoor area when possible for nature walks, etc. assuring adequate adult supervision.

FREE CHOICE CENTERS

Centers could be available for play during: Arrival, Departure, and Transitions, such as, in completing arts and crafts (Recommended 2-3 centers available at a time. Make more centers available for higher numbers of children in attendance.)

- **Word Wall:** children practice reading by placing the (teacher drawn) pictures and words in order from a Bible scripture related to the lesson, such as scripture from "What Did God Say" Follow up Activity.
- **Blocks:** (define the boundaries of the area, i.e. with masking tape; a shelf that holds the blocks could also be used as a boundary)
- **Board game:** for two to four children (think of ways to relate the children's play to what you want the children to learn)
- **Manipulative toys:** (such as puppets, Legos, small plastic animals, etc. can be used with the block play or separately)
- **Puzzles** (Lesson related)
- **Books** (Lesson related)
- **Coloring/ Drawing/ Cutting / Gluing** (Lesson related)
- **Dramatic Play**

POSITIVE GUIDANCE

As much as possible reinforce the behaviors you want to see repeated.

For example, if four children are present and are not paying attention, say to the one paying attention, "I like how (child's name) is sitting so nice and listening."

(The children want to hear that they are doing the right thing, so as each one sits correctly, let them know you like how they are sitting and listening also.)

DAILY SCHEDULE

(For Children's Church/ Part Day School Settings)
Adjust times to fit your schedule.

10:00 -10:30 .... ARRIVAL / FREE PLAY

10:30 – 10:35 .... TRANSITION TO CIRCLE

10:35–11:00 .... CIRCLE: SONGS/REVIEW OF DAY'S ACTIVITIES / SONG / STORY LESSON / CONVERSATIONS OF THANKS GIVING / PRAISE & WORSHIP / BIBLE SCRIPTURE

11:00- 11:05 .... TRANSITION TO TABLES / EXPLAIN CRAFT

11:05 – 11:30 .... FOLLOW-UP ACTIVITIES (ARTS AND CRAFTS)

11:30 – 11:35 .... CLEAN-UP/ RESTROOM / TRANSITION TO SNACK

11:35 – 11:50 .... PRAYER / SNACK / CLEAN-UP

11:50 - 12:00 .... FREE PLAY / PARENT PICK-UP

CHILDREN'S ARRIVAL/FREEPLAY

(Have some toys and games available for children to play freely when they enter the room. See free choice centers for ideas)

1) Teachers greet children and parents and briefly tell parents at least one of the objectives for their child to learn that day. (See Objectives for each story lesson on the STUDENT PROGRESS RECORD) (Example: Your child will be learning about CREATION, to understand that God is their heavenly Father.)

2) Teacher to guide child to choose someone to play with in a free play area until all children have arrived.

TRANSITION

Use Transition Songs to move children from one area to another.

For example, to transition the children from **Arrival/Free** Play to Circle on the carpet you begin by announcing to the children that they have 5 more minutes until clean up,

(then as time passes)
Announce 3 more minutes until clean up, and the 1 minute notice.
(By telling the children of the time left to play, you can avoid children not being ready to finish their play because they have had notice.)

When time is up, you can begin to sing the Clean up Song. Before clean up or as the children are putting toys away, let them know where you want them to go next, i.e. when you finish putting away your toys, come and sit quietly on the circle by the ...

(See SONGS FOR YOU TO SING WITH CHILDREN)
Modify the songs as needed to suit your transition or your theme, i.e.

Clean up, clean up!
We clean up messes everywhere!
Clean up, clean up!
We all pitch in and do our share!

CIRCLE

(These are simply suggestions of how to do circle. Be creative!)

- Sing songs to transition children to circle time. After children are in the circle area, you could begin with an introduction song.
  (See SONGS TO SING WITH CHILDREN)

- Tell the children about the day's activities they will do.
  (Ex. Today we are going to hear a story about how God, your heavenly Father made everything… and when we go to the tables you can make a … and…)

- Transition to the story with an expressive song/rhyme.
  (See SONGS FOR YOU TO SING WITH CHILDREN)

- Read the Foundation Curriculum Story Book lesson, i.e. "CREATION" showing the pictures, asking the questions engrafted into the story and listening to the answers.

- Initiate conversations about the Story Lesson as it relates to the children's personal lives.
  (Encourage children to talk about things in their lives they are thankful to Father for).
  Then encourage children to praise Father and thank Him and Jesus.

- Praise and Worship! Dance! Play musical instruments, etc.

- Bible Scripture on Word Wall: Post the words of a bible verse related to the Story Book Lesson.
  (You can find scriptures related to the Story Book Lesson you are teaching at the end of the Follow-Up Activities).
  Select one scripture and read the scripture to the children. Then scramble the words so the children can place the words in order.

- Sing a Song for children to go to Tables for Follow-up Activity.
  (See SONGS FOR YOU TO SING WITH CHILDREN)

FOLLOW-UP ACTIVITIES

To reinforce the objectives in each of the six **Foundation Curriculum** story book lessons, **Follow-Up** activities are provided. The Follow-Up include Activities such as, short teachings with art, songs, crafts, games and **role-play** to help **children** know the love of **God** as **Father**, **Jesus** as **Savior** and friend, and **Holy Spirit**. You can also creatively plan your own craft, art or game activity that help each child to understand the lesson objectives.

(As children finish activities before others, let them choose which free choice center they would like to quietly play in.)

CLEAN UP

As each child finishes, they are reminded to clean up and place their art/craft in the area designated by the teacher. Teacher reminds children of the Free Choice Centers where they can choose to play until all children finish with their follow-up activity.

(See free choice centers)
(Use clean up song as needed.)
(Transition to Bathroom/Hand washing.)
(Clean off tables for snack.)

RESTROOM/TRANSITION TO SNACK

After hand washing remind children to walk back to tables and be seated for snack.

(Select helpers to help set table for snack, such as, to put out napkins and cups)

PRAYER/SNACK/CLEAN-UP

Encourage children to pray and thank (heavenly) **Father** for our food. Let all **children** who choose to pray "**PRAY**", so that children learn to thank **Father** for all things. Eat with **children** and talk with them about topics such as, what they made for **art**, their **families**, their **pets**, the **Story Lesson**, etc.

FREEPLAY/PARENT PICK-UP

After **children** finish snack, they can choose to play in the **Free Choice Centers** until their parents arrive.

When starting a new **Foundation Curriculum** Story Book lesson, give each parent the appropriate "**Parent Letter**" for the book you are beginning.

(You could also run a copy of the Story Book Lesson text and a Follow-Up Activity to send home for parents to reinforce with their child.)

STUDENT PROGRESS RECORD

Set a time to **talk to parents** about the **Student Progress Record** and how you can work together to help their child meet the **goals** and **objectives** of the **curriculum**. Keep the **Student Progress Record** updated for each child. Show the parents the things you have seen and documented of the **child's spiritual growth**. Document the information the parents' provide of things the child has done at home that demonstrate an **objective** was **understood** by the child.

KINGDOM OF GOD RULE

LOVE EACH OTHER!

"I give you a new command: Love each other. You must love each other just as I loved you. All people will know that you are my followers if you love each other." JOHN 13:34-35 (ERV)

LOVE ONE ANOTHER AS JESUS LOVES YOU THAT IS WHAT JESUS TOLD FRIENDS TO DO.

QUESTIONS AND ANSWERS

QUESTIONS THAT YOU MAY HAVE ABOUT THE TEACHINGS AND THE ANSWERS FROM GOD'S WORD!

Did God make all people from the seed inside the first man?
Genesis 1:11-12 Then God said, Let the earth bring forth grass, the herb that yields seed, and the fruit tree that yields fruit according to its kind, whose seed is in itself, on the earth; and it was so. And the earth brought forth grass, the herb that yields seed according to its kind and the tree that yields fruit whose seed is in itself according to its kind. And God saw that it was good. (This is the first place in scripture where we see God command seed to be inside of the living thing that He creates so that it can yield seed and reproduce according to its kind. The next living things that He creates to be according to its kind, is sea creatures and birds. And just like the fruit tree whose seed is in itself, God blessed the sea creatures and birds and told them to be fruitful and multiply. See Genesis 1:20-22) In Genesis 1:24-25, God tells the earth to bring forth the living creature according to its kind. (The command to be fruitful comes with God placing the seed inside of the newly created living thing so that it can reproduce and be fruitful.) In Genesis 1:28 God blessed man and told them to be fruitful and multiply and fill the earth. Genesis 3:20 (NKJ) And Adam called his wife's name Eve because she was the mother of all living. It is written in Genesis 5:2, "Male and female created He them; and blessed them, and called their name Adam, in the day when they were created." KJV (Genesis 5:2 says that both Adam and Eve were called Adam by God; and Genesis 3:20 says 'all living' came from man (Adam and Eve) (Genesis 5 tells of the genealogy of Adam through Noah. Then after the flood, in Genesis 9:1 it says "So God blessed Noah and his sons, and said to them: Be fruitful and multiply, and fill the earth." (And from the sons of Noah, the descendants of the fruitful seed of Adam, the earth was filled again.) According to God's Word, Yes, God made all people from the seed inside the first man, Adam

Did God make you as a three part being (spirit, soul, and body?)
Genesis 2:7 And the LORD God formed man of the dust of the ground, and breathed into his nostrils the breath of life; and man became a living soul. (kjv) I Thessalonians 5:23, says "Now may the God of peace Himself sanctify you completely; and may your whole spirit, soul and body be preserved blameless at the coming of our Lord Jesus Christ". Hebrews 4:12 says "For the Word of God is living and powerful, and sharper than any two edged sword, piercing even to the division of soul and spirit and of joints and marrow…" Ecclesiastes 12:7 says "Then the dust will return to the earth as it was, and the spirit will return to God who gave it". Jesus said in Matthew 10:28, "And do not fear those who kill the body but cannot kill the soul. But rather fear Him who is able to destroy both soul and body in hell". Romans 8:16, "the Spirit Himself bears witness with our spirit that we are children of God". According to God's Word, these six scriptures testify to the affirmative that Yes, God made man as a three part being of spirit, soul and body.

Is it true that your soul lives forever either in a good place called heaven or a bad place called hell?
John 3:16 says, "For God so loved the world that He gave His only begotten Son that whoever believes in Him should not perish but have everlasting life." Daniel 12:2 said "And many of those who sleep in the dust of the earth shall awake. Some to everlasting life, Some to shame and everlasting contempt." Jesus said in Matthew 10:28, "And do not fear those who kill the body but cannot kill the soul. But rather fear Him who is able to destroy both soul and body in hell." 2 Thessalonians 1:9 "These shall be punished with everlasting destruction from the presence of the Lord and from the glory of His power" Revelation 21:7-8 says "He who overcomes shall inherit all things, and I will be his God and he shall be My son. But the cowardly, unbelieving, abominable, murderers, sexually immoral, sorcerers, idolaters, and all liars shall have their part in the lake of fire and brimstone, which is the second death." The Word of God says it's true, our souls are everlasting and some will have everlasting life with Father in heaven, and some to shame and everlasting destruction.

Is it true you can choose to speak in an unknown tongue?

From creation, God our Father gave man choice. When God gave Adam the command that he could eat from every tree in the garden; but not to eat from the tree of the knowledge of good and evil, Genesis 2:16-17 Adam chose to disobey. Genesis 3:6 God said in Deuteronomy 30:19 "I call heaven and earth as witnesses today against you. I have set before you life and death, blessing and cursing: therefore choose life, that both you and your descendants may live.." In Deuteronomy 30:20, God our Father continues speaking to tell us why we should choose to obey Him, saying, "that you may love the LORD your God, that you may obey His voice, and that you may cling to Him, for He is your life and the length of your days; and that you may dwell in the land which the LORD swore to your fathers, to Abraham, Isaac, and Jacob to give them." In Ephesians 6:10 we are told to be strong in the Lord and in the power of His might. (*That's a choice you make – To be strong in the Lord's strength or to do it your own way.*) In Ephesians 6:11 We are told to "put on the whole armor of God that you may be able to stand against the wiles of the devil". (*Again that's a choice you make – you can either put on the whole armor of God, put on part of it, or put on none of it.*) Ephesians 6:12 – 18 tells us why we should put on the whole armor of God and describes the armor. In Ephesians 6:18 we are told to always pray with all prayer and supplication in the Spirit. We are told that in order to stand against the trickery of the devil, to pray in the Spirit. Ephesians 6:11, 18 To always pray with all prayer and supplication in the Spirit is a choice. The Word of God instructs us to pray in the Spirit. Ephesians 6:18 In I Corinthians 14:18, the writer Paul says, "I thank my God I speak with tongues more than you all." (Paul chose to pray in tongues.) The Word of God says in I Corinthians 14:14 For if I pray in a tongue, my spirit prays, but my understanding is unfruitful. (This scripture says that when you pray in a tongue your spirit prays.) Our God and Father is good, kind, full of love, compassion and mercy. He does not tell us to do something that we cannot choose to do. God, our Father gives us choice, and His instruction is always for our good. But it's *our choice* to obey *or* to disobey. Deuteronomy 30:19

Is it true that when you were born again, that you are born again by the good seed in Jesus?

Jesus said in John 3:6-7 "That which is born of the flesh is flesh, and that which is born of the Spirit is spirit. Do not marvel that I said to you, You must be born again." I Peter 1:23 says "having been born again not of corruptible seed but incorruptible through the Word of God which lives and abides forever." The Holy Scripture says that we were born again of incorruptible seed through the Word of God. I Peter 1:23 Revelation 19:13 and John 1:1-4 says and describes Jesus as the Word of God. We were born again of seed that does not decay, corrupt or is immortal. (The New Strong's Exhaustive Concordance of the Bible, Greek: 862, incorruptible) In Matthew 13:37, Jesus said, "He who sows the good seed is the Son of Man." (Jesus said seed singular, not plural. Jesus called Himself the Son of man (see Matthew 9:6; 10:23).) Jesus, as the Son of man sows the good seed. Matthew 13:37 Jesus said in Luke 8:11 "the seed is the Word of God." According to the Word of God, when you were born again, it was of incorruptible seed that Jesus sowed. I Peter 1:23 And the seed that Jesus sowed for you to be born again of the Spirit is good seed. John 3:6-7 Jesus sowed *His life* as seed for you to born again. Isaiah 53:10-12

Is it true that your born again Spirit looks like heavenly Father and Jesus?

Hebrews 1:3 says about Jesus, "who being the brightness of His glory and the express image of His person.." Colossians 1:15 says "He is the image of the Invisible God, the firstborn over all creation." Also see 2 Corinthians 4:4; (These scriptures say that Jesus is the image of God) Romans 8:29 says, "For who He foreknew, He also predestined *to be* conformed to the image of His Son that He might be the firstborn among many brethren." I Corinthians 15:49 says "And as we have borne the image of the *man* of dust, we shall also bear the image of the heavenly *Man*. (These two scriptures confirm our spiritual man is in the image of Jesus.) Jesus is in the image of Father. Hebrew 1:3, Colossians 1:15; John 4:24 And man's born again spirit is in the image of Jesus and Father which is the original plan of God in Genesis 1:26-27.

Is it true that sin is no longer a problem because of Jesus?

In John 1:29 when John the Baptist saw Jesus coming toward him, John said, "Behold the Lamb of God who takes away the sin of the world. Romans 3:20-26 says "Therefore by the deeds of the law no flesh will be justified in His sight, for by the law is the knowledge of sin. But now the righteousness of God apart from the law is revealed, being witnessed by the Law and the Prophets, even the righteousness of God, through faith in Jesus Christ, to all and on all who believe. For there is no difference, for all have sinned and fall short of the glory of God; being justified freely by His grace through the redemption that is in Christ Jesus; whom God set forth as a propitiation by His blood, through faith, to demonstrate His righteousness because in His forbearance God had passed over the sins that were previously committed, to demonstrate at the present time His righteousness that He might be just and the justifier of the one who has faith in Jesus." (These scriptures say that the law gave people knowledge of sin. But God sent Jesus to atone and make payment in full for the sins of all men. And that God is a justifier of those who believe that Jesus took care of sin by His blood. I John 2:1-2; 4:10) Romans 6:10-12 speaking of Jesus says that He died to sin once for all but the life that He lives, He lives to God. Likewise you also reckon yourselves to be dead indeed to sin, but alive to God in Christ Jesus our Lord. Therefore do not let sin reign in your mortal body that you should obey it in its lusts. I John 1:6 says "If we say we have fellowship with Him and walk in darkness, we lie and do not practice the truth. (The truth is that the world was justified when Jesus died to sin once for all. But everyone still has to choose to believe Jesus and practice the truth of living unto God.) I John 1:7 says, "But if we walk in the light as He is in the light, we have fellowship with one another, and the blood of Jesus Christ His Son cleanses us from all sin."

Is it true that when you believe Jesus, you can use the name of Jesus to heal the sick?

In John 14:12-14 Jesus said, "Most assuredly I say to you, he who believes in Me, the works that I do he will do also, and greater works than these he will do because I go to My Father. And whatever you ask in My name that I will do that the Father may be glorified in the Son. If you ask anything in My name I will do *it*." Jesus said in Mark 16:15-18, "Go into all the world and preach the gospel to every creature. He who believes and is baptized will be saved. But he who does not believe will be condemned. And these signs will follow those who believe: In My name they will cast out demons; they will speak with new tongues; they will take up serpents; and if they drink anything deadly, it will by no means hurt them; they will lay hands on the sick and they will recover." Yes, Jesus said, those who believe Him can use His name to heal the sick.

Is receiving Holy Spirit separate from receiving Jesus in your heart?

In John 3:5 Jesus is having a conversation with Nicodemus. Jesus tells Nicodemus that "unless one is born of water and the Spirit, he cannot enter the Kingdom of God. That which is born of the flesh is flesh and that which is born of the Spirit is spirit." The conversation continues with Nicodemus, and Jesus said, "And as Moses lifted up the serpent in the wilderness even so must the Son of Man be lifted up, that whoever believes in Him should not perish but have eternal life. John 3:14-15 Later Jesus was talking to the Samaritan woman saying, "If you knew the gift of God, and who it is who says to you, Give Me a drink, you would have asked Him, and He would have given you living water. John 4:10) In John 4:14 Jesus said to her," but whoever drinks of the water that I shall give him will never thirst. But the water that I shall give him will become in him a fountain of water springing up into everlasting life." John 7:37-39 Jesus stood and cried out, "If anyone thirsts, let him come to Me and drink. He who believes in Me, as the Scripture has said, out of his heart will flow rivers of living water." ("But this He spoke concerning the Spirit, whom those believing in Him would receive; for the Holy Spirit was not yet *given*, because Jesus was not yet glorified."(John 7:39) John 20:21-22 After being raised from the dead by Holy Spirit, Jesus came to the disciples and said, "Peace to you! As the Father has sent Me, I also send you." Jesus breathed on them and said, "Receive the Holy Spirit." (His disciples had walked with Jesus on the earth and participated in His ministry. They were saved.) Yet in Acts 1:4, 5, 8 before Jesus ascended to heaven to be with His Father again, He said to His disciples who already believed Him, to wait for the Promise of the Father…"For John truly baptized with water, but you shall be baptized with the Holy Spirit not many days from now…But you shall receive power when the Holy Spirit has come upon you; and you shall be witnesses to Me in Jerusalem and in all Judea and Samaria, and to the end of the earth." (The disciples of Jesus that already believed Him and were saved/had eternal life, but they still prayed for the promise of the Father that Jesus spoke of--for the Holy Spirit to be sent to earth. Also awaiting the Holy Spirit's arrival was Mary, the mother of Jesus and His brothers. Acts 1:14 Acts 2:1-4 described what happened when the Holy Spirit arrived on earth on the Day of Pentecost, "And they were all filled with the Holy Spirit and began to speak with other tongues, as the Spirit gave them utterance." In Acts 8:5-13 Phillip preached to the Samaritans and the multitudes in the city believed Jesus and were saved/had eternal life, and received baptism in water. However Acts 8:14-17 says

"Now when the apostles who were at Jerusalem heard that Samaria had received the word of God, they sent Peter and John to them, who when they had come down prayed for them that they might receive the Holy Spirit. For as yet He had fallen upon none of them. They had only been baptized in the name of the Lord Jesus. Then they laid hands on them and they received the Holy Spirit." When we believe in Jesus, by faith, we are saved and have eternal life, and are cleaned, and sanctified with the washing of water by His Word. John 5:24; 15:3; Romans 10:8-13; John 15:3; Ephesians 5:26 We are born again of God, as His children, when we receive the baptism with the Holy Spirit. John 1:12-13; 1:33, 3:5; 7:37-39 And we are called to practice righteousness as born again children of God. John 3:20-21; Romans 8; I John 3:10

What if someone does not receive the gift of speaking in tongues?
In I Corinthians 14:1-2, the Word of God said to "pursue love and desire spiritual *gifts*..." "For he who speaks in a tongue does not speak to men but to God, for no one understands *him*; however in the spirit he speaks mysteries." Jude 1:20 says "But you beloved, building yourself up on your most holy faith, praying in the Holy Spirit." Romans 8:26-28 says "Likewise the Spirit also helps in our weaknesses. For we do not know what we should pray for as we ought, but the Spirit Himself makes intercession for us with groaning which cannot be uttered. Now He who searches the heart knows what the mind of the Spirit *is*, because He makes intercession for the saints according to *the will of* God. And we know that all things work together for good to those who love God to those who are the called according to *His* purpose. How then can a compassionate God and Father make available such a great help for His children and not let them receive it? It's available to all who desire it. I Corinthians 14:1; Psalm 37:4 Ask for it. Matthew 7:7-11 Believe your Father loves you and wants you to have His gift. Luke 11:13   For the Word of God says, "For if I pray in a tongue, my spirit prays but my understanding is unfruitful..." I Corinthians 14:14   Begin by faith to believe God and focus on Him -- then speak the sounds from your heart and pray to Father. Do not think about the sounds with your mind. I Corinthians 14:14   Like a baby just learning to speak, each time you speak to your Father in the Spirit, your language will get clearer, but your Father hears and understands you. I Corinthians 14:2 It is a person's choice to receive Father's free gift or to reject it.

What does God's Word say about Receiving Communion?

In Luke 22:17-20 it says about Jesus, "Then He took the cup, and gave thanks and said, Take this and divide it among yourselves; for I say to you, I will not drink of the fruit of the vine until the kingdom of God comes," And He took bread, gave thanks and broke it and gave it to them saying, "This is My body which is given for you; do this in remembrance of Me." Likewise He took the cup after supper saying, "This cup is the new covenant in My blood, which is shed for you." Mark 14:22-26 described the Lord's Supper saying, "And as they were eating, Jesus took bread, blessed and broke it, and gave it to them and said, "Take eat. This is My body." Then He took the cup and when He had given thanks He gave it to them and they all drank from it. And He said to them, "This is My blood of the new covenant, which is shed for many. Assuredly I say to you, I will no longer drink of the fruit of the vine until that day when I drink it new in the Kingdom of God." And when they had sung a hymn, they went out to the Mount of Olives." Jesus instructs His disciples (learners and pupils*) to take and eat the bread to remember that He gave His body for us; and to drink from the cup of His blood of our new covenant with God, to remember that He shed His blood for the remission of sins. (*The Strong's Exhaustive Concordance of the Bible: Greek meaning of disciples 3101) To receive communion is an act of obedience to remember what our Lord has done by physically shedding His blood and giving His body for our redemption. In gratitude we symbolically eat the bread in representation of His body and drink fruit juice to symbolize His bloodshed for us. The Word of God cautions those who take communion to examine themselves as to not take the communion in an unworthy manner for there is judgment in dishonoring our Lord's sacrifice. (I Corinthians 11:17-34)

Does God always heal when we put our hands on and believe?

The Word of God says, And these signs shall follow those who believe….they will lay hands on the sick and they will recover." Mark 16:17-18 Psalm 89:34 "My covenant I will not break, nor alter the Word that has gone out of My lips." Titus 1:2 speaks saying, "in hope of eternal life which God who cannot lie promised…" God cannot lie and He spoke His Word through Jesus. John 12:50 In Matthew 17:14-21 the disciples of Jesus could not heal an epileptic boy, but Jesus healed the boy by rebuking the demon that was in the child. The disciples came to Jesus in private and asked Him, "why could we not cast it out?" Jesus said to them, "Because of your unbelief. For assuredly, I say to you, if you have faith as a mustard seed, you will say to this mountain, Move from here to there, and it will move; and nothing will be impossible for you. However this kind does not go out except by prayer and fasting." The Word of God is true and God always does what He says He will do.

HOLY BIBLE SCRIPTURE REFERENCES

"CREATION" SCRIPTURE REFERENCES

Matthew 6:9 Jesus said to pray to God as "Our Father."
Psalm 11:4 Father's throne is in heaven.
Isaiah 57:15 Father's name and His dwelling place is holy.
Matthew 5:48 Father is perfect.
Isaiah 45:19 Father does all things right.
Isaiah 44:6 There is no other God.
John 17:23 Father loves you just like He loves Jesus.
John 4:24 God, our heavenly Father is a Spirit.
Luke 24:39 A Spirit does not have flesh and bones.
Matthew 19:17 God is good.
Hebrews 6:18; Titus 1:2   It is impossible for God to lie.
Philippians 4:6 Father wants us to pray to Him about everything. He wants you to ask and to thank Him.
I John 4:8 God is Love!
Genesis 1:3; 1:6-7; 1:9; 1:11; 1:14-15; 1:20-22; 1:24; 1:26-28;1:29-30 God spoke Words and created and made all things alive.
John 6:63 God's Words are Spirit and life.
Hebrews 4:12 God's Word is living and powerful.
Genesis 1:1-5 This is what God Created on Day 1.

"CREATION" SCRIPTURE REFERENCES (CONTINUED):

Genesis 1:6-8 This is what God Created on Day 2.
Genesis 1:9-13 This is what God Created on Day 3.
Genesis 1:14-19 This is what God Created on Day 4.
Genesis 1:20-23 This is what God Created on Day 5.
Genesis 1:24-31 This is what God Created on Day 6.
Genesis 1:26-27 Male and female were made to look like (resemble) and be like (a representative of) God, our Father, Jesus and Holy Spirit. (You were made to look like love.)
Matthew 22:36-40; John 15:12 Mankind is commanded to love; to love God first with all our heart, soul and mind, and; to love one another as He has loved us.
Genesis 1:28 God blessed the first man and woman to be fruitful and multiply (to fill the earth with children in the image and likeness of God).
Genesis 1:28 God gave mankind dominion over the earth to rule.
Matthew 13:38 The good seeds are the sons of the Kingdom of Father.
Genesis 2:2 God rested on the 7th day.
Hebrews 4:3-6 God rested, and man could choose to enter into God's rest by trusting and believing Him.
Proverbs 12:18 Mankind was made to speak words that give life.
I Corinthians 13:4-8 is God's kind of love to us and how we are to love each other.
Jeremiah 9:23-24 God wants mankind to understand and know Him.
Psalm 145:21 We can praise our Father with the words we speak.
Psalm 150 Let everything that has breathe Praise the Lord!!!

"THE FALL OF MAN" SCRIPTURE REFERENCES

Matthew 6:10 Jesus told us to pray for Father's Will to be done on earth as it is in heaven.
Isaiah 44:6 There is one God.
I John 4:8 God is love.
Psalm 11:4 Father's throne is in heaven.
Genesis 6:2 Angels can choose.
Job 1:6 God called angels His sons.
Isaiah 14:12-20 Lucifer wanted to be like God.
Revelation 12:7-9; Luke 10:18 Lucifer fought the good angels and lost and was kicked out of heaven.
Genesis 1:28 God gave the earth to (Adam) mankind to rule.
Genesis 1:26-28 God made man to be like Him.
John 4:24 God is a Spirit.
Genesis 2:7 God formed a body for Adam's spirit.
I Thessalonians 5:23 God made us in three parts - spirit, soul, and body.
Deuteronomy 30:19 God gave man the ability to choose to obey or disobey Him so that man and his seed may live.
Genesis 2:8 God planted a garden.
Genesis 2:17 God commanded and warned Adam not to eat from the tree of the knowledge of good and evil because death would come the day he ate of it.
Genesis 3:1 satan came into the garden as a snake.
John 8:44 satan, the devil always tells lies.

P.A.C.E.
www.ABC-Jesus.com
© All Rights Reserved

"THE FALL OF MAN" SCRIPTURE REFERENCES (CONTINUED):

Genesis 3:6 Adam and Eve disobeyed God.
Romans 6:16 God's law of whoever you obey rules you.
Titus 1:2 God cannot lie.
Romans 5:12 Death came into the world.
Genesis 3:24 Adam and Eve had to leave the garden.
Genesis 3:15, John 3:16 God planned to send Jesus.
Genesis 4:1 Adam and Eve had children.
Genesis 6:5 Most of Adam's children thought, spoke, and did evil.
Deuteronomy 30:19 God wants you to choose His kingdom of love!

"JESUS" SCRIPTURE REFERENCES

Matthew 6:11	Jesus told us to pray give us this day our daily bread.
Genesis 2:17	Adam was not to eat from a certain tree.
Genesis 3:6	Adam did not believe God and disobeyed.
Romans 5:12	Sickness and death came on earth.
Matthew 4:8-9	The earth had become the devil's kingdom.
Romans 6:23; 7:25	The law of sin and death was activated that day.
John 3:16; 8:32-34	Father loves you so much He sent His Son Jesus to save you.
John 6:32-35	Jesus came from heaven to die in your place.
Galatians 3:19	Jesus is the seed Father promised in Genesis 3:15
I Peter 1:23	Father put His good seed in Jesus for you to be born again in Jesus.
Luke 5:13; Luke 4:35; Matthew 9:24-25	Jesus healed the sick, made devils leave, and dead people come to life.
Matthew 27:22-23	Some people hated and did not believe Jesus.
Matthew 27:26-31	People whipped and tortured Jesus.
Isaiah 52:14	Jesus body was beat so badly he did not look human.
Luke 23:34	On the cross Jesus prayed for Father to forgive the people.
Matthew 27:35; 27:50	People killed the Son of the Most High God by crucifixion.
Isaiah 53:4-5; I Peter 2:24	You were made whole by what Jesus suffered for you.
I Peter 3:18	Jesus body died but His Spirit was alive.
Colossians 2:15	The Spirit of Jesus went to hell and beat up satan and his devils.
Revelation 1:18	Jesus took the keys of hell and death.

"JESUS" SCRIPTURE REFERENCES (CONTINUED):

Romans 8:11 Father raised Jesus from hell by Holy Spirit.
Hebrews 9:12 Father has forgiven you because Jesus shed his blood for us all.
John 3:3-8 You can be born again by the good seed in Jesus.
2 Corinthians 5:17-18 Your born again spirit will be a new creation in Jesus.
I Peter 3:22 Jesus went home to His Father.
John 17:3 You can live forever and know and understand Father and Jesus.
Romans 10:9-10 You can pray and ask Father to forgive and save you.
I Thessalonians 5:18 You can thank Father and Jesus for what they did for you!
John 14:16-17 Jesus wants you to receive gift of Holy Spirit.
I Corinthians 14:2 Holy Spirit will help you pray to Father in a special language.
I Corinthians 14:2 Holy Spirit will help you pray to Father in a special language.
Luke 11:13 You can ask Father to give you Holy Spirit.
Matthew 6:6 You can find a secret place to pray to Father.

"FORGIVE" SCRIPTURE REFERENCES

Luke 11:4 Jesus said to pray and speak forgive our sins just as we forgive everyone who has done wrong to us.
Romans 5:12-19 Sin and death entered the world through Adam, but you were redeemed by Jesus.
John 3:3-8 You can be born again, in your spirit into the kingdom of God as a child of Father.
2 Corinthians 5:17 when you receive Jesus you are a new creation.
John 13:15 Jesus is our example of how to live as God's child.
Ephesians 4:22-24 You must learn to think and do things new, like Jesus.
Acts 1:8; Luke 3:22 You can receive super power of Holy Spirit like Jesus.
John 14:16-17 Holy Spirit will help you like He helped Jesus.
2 Timothy 1:7 You have nothing to fear when you have God's power of Holy Spirit.
Deuteronomy 30:19 You must choose who you will obey.
Genesis 3:5-6 Adam and Eve chose to obey the devil.
Philippians 2:8-9; John 10:17-18 Father has highly exalted the name of Jesus because Jesus chose to give His life for you.
Revelation 17:14 Father made Jesus King of kings.
2 Corinthians 5:18-21 Jesus wants you to be a king and ambassador on earth for Him.
Luke 23:34 To be like Jesus you must show love and forgive everyone.
2 Corinthians 2:10-11 when you do not forgive, you allow satan to take advantage of you.
Matthew 6:6-13; Luke 11:1-4 Praying to Father, like Jesus, is your secret weapon.
John 14:26 Holy Spirit is your Helper to help you forgive and do all things in love.

"FORGIVE" SCRIPTURE REFERENCES (CONTINUED):

Romans 12:19-21 When you show love, God takes care of your enemies.
Matthew 6:14-15 If you do not forgive others Father will not forgive you.
Matthew 5:44-48 You are Father's child, leader, and ambassador to show others His love on earth, like Jesus!

"YOUR POWER IN JESUS" SCRIPTURE REFERENCES

Matthew 6:13 Jesus said to pray and say lead us not into temptation but deliver us from the evil one.
2 Corinthians 5:17 When you received Jesus you became a new creation.
Romans 12:2 We must learn to do things like our Father and Jesus
Genesis 1:26-28 We were made to be like Father, Jesus and Holy Spirit.
Genesis 1 God spoke words that gave life.
Proverbs 18:21 God put great power of death and life in the words we speak.
Proverbs 2:1-12 Father wants us to speak good words that give life.
Proverbs 6:2 The power in the bad words you speak entangle you.
Deuteronomy 30:19 God gave you the power to choose (you can choose to say words that give life or words the devil can use to bring death).
John 6:63 Your words are spirit. You cannot see them.
Ephesians 6:12 The battle we fight on earth is spiritual.
2 Corinthians 10:3-5 A spiritual weapon to use in battle is to cast away every thought that goes against words Jesus spoke.
John 8:44 The devil is the father of lies and will try to get you to receive words that are lies from him like he did Adam and Eve in Genesis 3:5.
John 14:17; Acts 1:8 Holy Spirit is the bigger and greater power from God, and can be with us to help us when we believe Jesus.
2 Corinthians 10:3-6 You can examine every thought and change bad thoughts to good.
Proverbs 23:7 As you think your words and actions follow.
Philippians 4:8-9 You can practice thinking kind and good thoughts.

"YOUR POWER IN JESUS" SCRIPTURE REFERNECES (CONTINUED):

Ephesians 6:17 When you believe and speak Words God spoke you have pulled out a sword that the enemy cannot stand against.
Ephesians 6:18 Pray always in the Spirit and with words that God has said.
Psalm 149:6-9 Let the high praises of God be in their mouth, and a two-edged sword in their hand.
Matthew 6:13 Jesus said to pray and say for Yours is the Kingdom, and the power and the glory forever. Amen.
Revelation 4:11 God created all things.
Isaiah 66:1 God's throne is in heaven.

"THE KINGDOM OF GOD" SCRIPTURE REFERENCE"

I John 4:8 God is love.
James 2:8 God's royal law is to love.
John 1:4-5; Revelation 21:23 God is life and light.
Psalm 89:5-18 Father rules the universe.
Revelation 19:15 God is Almighty.
Acts 1:11 Jesus lives with His Father in heaven.
John 14:2 Jesus is preparing big houses in heaven for God's children.
Revelation 22:1-2 The River of Life flows in heaven.
Revelation 4:3 There are bright colors and rainbows in heaven.
Revelation 21:18-21 There are many jewels in heaven.
Revelation 6:2 There are horses in heaven.
John 8:28-29 Jesus came to earth and did everything His Father told Him.
Philippians 2:9-11 Father gave Jesus a name above all names filled with His power.
John 14:12-14 Jesus gave all who believe Him the authority to use His name to do the works He did and greater.
Matthew 9:35 Jesus taught the people about the kingdom of God.
Mark 1:34; 5:39-42 Jesus cured sick people, made demons leave, and raised the dead.
Matthew 10:1; Luke 10:1-17 Jesus showed His followers how to do the things He did.

"THE KINGDOM OF GOD" SCRIPTURE REFERENCES (CONTINUED):

Mark 16:15-20 Jesus has made you His ambassador to tell and show people on earth the kingdom of heaven.
John 14:13-15 You can give Father glory when you obey Him and love like Jesus.
John 17:22-23 Jesus gave you His glory for the purpose of being One with Him and Father and to let the world know Father sent Jesus.

www.ingramcontent.com/pod-product-compliance
Lightning Source LLC
Chambersburg PA
CBHW041513220426
43668CB00002B/12